STILL
THROWING
HEAT

Strikeouts, the Streets,
and a Second Chance

J. R. Richard
with Lew Freedman

TRIUMPH
BOOKS

Library of Congress Cataloging-in-Publication Data
Richard, J. R., 1950–
  Still throwing heat : strikeouts, the streets, and a second chance / J. R. Richard, Lew Freedman ; foreword by Nolan Ryan.
    pages cm
  ISBN 978-1-62937-099-6 (hardback)
1. Richard, J. R., 1950- 2. Baseball players—United States—Biography. 3. Pitchers (Baseball)—United States—Biography. 4. Cerebrovascular disease—Patients—Biography. I. Freedman, Lew. II. Title.
  GV865.R4275A3 2015
  796.357092—dc23
  [B]   2014049339

This book is available in quantity at special discounts for your group or organization. For further information, contact:
  Triumph Books LLC
  814 North Franklin Street
  Chicago, Illinois 60610
  (312) 337-0747
  www.triumphbooks.com

Printed in U.S.A.

ISBN: 978-1-62937-099-6

Design by Sue Knopf

Photos courtesy of Getty Images unless otherwise indicated

I dedicate this book to the Trinity—the Father, the Son, and the Holy Spirit—the Houston Astros, and all of the people who made it possible for me to write this book. I want to thank everyone who has helped me, especially my wife, Lula.

Contents

Foreword

I came to the Houston Astros from the California Angels for the 1980 season, and J.R. Richard was the mainstay of the starting rotation at the time. He was coming off a stretch where he had won between 18 and 20 games for four straight years and he was at the top of his game.

At the time we were both probably among the hardest throwing pitchers in the major leagues, and for the Astros, having us both in the rotation meant that opposing hitters were going to have to face two guys who threw their fastballs about 100 mph. That's a tough task for any team to take on.

The Astros were born as a National League expansion team in 1962 as the Houston Colt .45s. They changed the team's nickname to Astros after three seasons. When a team begins its life as an expansion team—mostly with players that other teams don't want—it is a given that it will probably be stuck at the bottom of the standings for a little while. The Houston club did start out that way. The Astros suffered through a bunch of eighth, ninth, and 10th-place finishes.

But when I signed with the Astros as a free agent in November of 1979, the team was on its way up. Houston had finished in second place in its division with an 89–73 record. The team had added young talent like J.R. Richard and for the first time believed that it could win a pennant. The fans started believing, too, and the franchise drew 1.9 million spectators that season.

Being from Texas, it appealed to me to play for a Texas team and it seemed as if I was joining Houston at just the right time. My judgment proved correct because the 1980 season was a breakthrough for the club.

And as well as J.R. had been pitching over the last several seasons, he seemed to reach a new peak in his performance in 1980. At 6'8" and 220 pounds, J.R. was a mammoth man. Combine that with his speed on his fastball, and he was very intimidating to hitters. There was less focus on radar guns during games 35 years ago, but we knew that we both threw at about 100 miles an hour, and that could seem overpowering to other teams.

In 1980 J.R. put together a tremendous first half of the season. He was chosen for the All-Star team for the first time in his career and earned the opportunity to be the National League starter. After just 17 starts that season, J.R. had a 10–4 record. But even that did not truly illustrate his effectiveness. J.R. had pitched 113⅔ innings and surrendered only 65 hits. That is a phenomenal rate. He had given up just 24 earned runs.

A year before, J.R. led the National League in earned run average with a 2.71 figure. Halfway through the 1980 season, his ERA was 1.90. He had been the best in the league in 1979 and had cut his ERA by almost a run a game.

That showed how much he had matured as a pitcher. A lot of fastball pitchers—and I was one of them—have trouble with control and walk a lot of guys when they are young. J.R. had gone through that, leading the league in walks three times. But in those 113 innings that season, J.R. had only allowed 40 walks.

It is fair to say that J.R. was one of the best pitchers in baseball when he was felled by a stroke. To see an athlete sidelined in such a manner when he is only 30 years old and is playing better than ever was *shocking*. It is sad enough if a star pitcher goes down with an arm injury. At least you can understand how that happens. For it to turn out that J.R. suffered a life-threatening stroke was devastating for everyone. Losing J.R. at that point in the season was a stunning thing for the Astros. We had the best team in club history. That team had a pitching rotation that was built to win it all. J.R. and I were joined by Joe Niekro, Ken Forsch, and Vern Ruhle. It was not one of my best seasons, but it was Vern's best.

Cesar Cedeno, Joe Morgan, Enos Cabell, and Jose Cruz were some of our best hitters. We were able to adjust and still finish 93–70 despite losing J.R. The season came down to the last game of the season for us to qualify for the National League Championship Series. In fact it took us one extra day because we were tied with the Los Angeles Dodgers for first in the National League West. We beat L.A. in a one-game playoff and faced the Philadelphia Phillies.

Philadelphia beat us and went on to win the World Series. It is always a tough thing to assume things in hindsight, but if we had a healthy J.R. Richard down the stretch and in the playoffs, it is possible that it would have been Houston and not Philadelphia winning the series in 1980.

Worst of all, J.R.'s career was over. A man who had been such a star at mid-season never pitched in the majors again. I feel confident in saying that if J.R. Richard had remained healthy he would have been an ace pitcher on the Astros for years to come.

—*Nolan Ryan*

Introduction

To me, J.R. Richard was a ghost with a reputation. I mostly lived in American League towns or towns with no Major League Baseball at all during his pitching era. I followed the game as best I could wherever I was, but J.R. and I only overlapped with the National League in 1980. Then he very much surfaced in my baseball viewing as the real deal since I had become a close NL observer through the Philadelphia Phillies.

J.R. Richard was one of the finest pitchers around. And in 1980 it was impossible to escape news about the fire-balling right-hander. First, it was the good kind of news. Richard was off to the best start of his career and was putting up staggering numbers. Then he was the starting pitcher for the NL in the All-Star Game.

After then the news wasn't so good. It was confusing, then depressing. Richard was felled by a mysterious illness, and the great pitcher could no longer pitch. From afar information was less available than it was in Houston—and even there it was difficult to digest and comprehend.

It must be remembered that this was an era when ESPN was in its infancy. Technology that sports fans routinely consult in 2015 was unknown 35 years earlier. Yes, baseball fans did hear periodic reports about Richard, but there was little context. We were rooting for him to make a comeback, as if he had simply torn a knee ligament, but we really didn't have a clear sense of what was going on with Richard's life.

Still, I always remembered his story, how terrific a pitcher he was, and how sadly his career had ended. I periodically read a nugget or two about J.R.'s life, and the spark of wanting to know more was rekindled. As a devotee of baseball history, I thought to reach out to J.R. and see if he would like to write a book about his life. But no one came to mind who would be a natural intermediary to put me in touch with J.R.

Eventually, an unexpected source, an old friend in Alaska named Don Hancock, who operates a sports memorabilia store and card shop in Anchorage, mentioned that J.R. Richard was scheduled to sign autographs in his store soon. I blurted out, "Ask him if he would like to do a book and how to get in touch with him." Don did, and J.R. and I got together, our conversations expanding into this volume.

Two things struck me about J.R. Richard the pitcher. One was how tall he was—6'8"—since pitchers did not tend to be built like basketball forwards at that time. The other was how fast he threw. It was the sound of the smack of the ball into the catcher's mitt that would snap your head around for a look as if you had just heard a gunshot. Those watching knew the real word to describe what they had just heard in the second or so before the collision of ball and glove was "Whoosh!" That's almost a cartoon sound, but the point is made.

J.R. Richard was blessed with great athletic talent. During his youth in Ruston, Louisiana, he developed his skills as a baseball, football, and basketball star. It was as if God reached down, touched him with a finger on his shoulder, and anointed him a chosen one.

Richard's former Astros teammates remember those days with fondness. Some of them recalled how the best hitters in the National League would quake as they stepped into the batter's box, wondering just how they would ever place their bats on the ball. Those teammates chuckled at the memories he made, claiming that some hitters would suddenly develop headaches or other illnesses on the days Richard was scheduled to pitch and take the day off altogether. That's how good he was.

By 1980, when Richard turned 30, he was in his prime, at the top of his game. By July Richard was 10–4 with a 1.90 ERA and was the NL starter in the All-Star Game. The man was on fire. An artist's rendition of Richard's follow-through might well have been depicted with flames shooting out of his arm like the expelled exhaust from a rocket ship. He was throwing a four-alarm fastball.

And then suddenly, he wasn't. In one of the strangest twists afflicting any baseball star's career, seemingly out of nowhere this bull of a man, this harnesser of great power, was struck by an inexplicable illness that at first was vague and then diagnosed as a stroke. *A stroke!* It seemed impossible.

Although our discussions were at times melancholy, I found J.R. Richard to be good company, fun to talk baseball with, someone with a good sense of humor, and a man remarkably free of bitterness considering the ordeal that destroyed his baseball career and life.

To hear out J.R. Richard, as I have, is to listen to the story of a great baseball player, but also the story of the redemption and rejuvenation of a life. J.R. is a man who serves as a terrific example for those who have faced hardships and conquered them. It is hard not to be as impressed with the senior citizen Richard as it was when he was clocking those blurring fastballs. It has been an epic journey for J.R. Richard, but he faces the world now as a man whose soul is rested.

—Lew Freedman

1

Emergency in the Astrodome

Soon after J.R. Richard rejoined the Houston Astros for the second half of the 1980 baseball season, he didn't feel well. He couldn't quite put his finger on what was wrong. Athletes know their bodies as well as anyone, and this indefinable problem got on Richard's nerves. He tried to dismiss it as nothing.

Though he was a premier pitcher who had the strength to overpower most batters with his 100 mph fastball, Richard felt that he was weakening in some ways. He wasn't pitching complete games during the stretch leading up to the All-Star break. He was getting fantastic results—wins, strikeouts, ERA, across the board—so any suggestion of injury was counterintuitive. As a self-described loner on the team, Richard did not confide in many Astros. His friend Enos Cabell, the third baseman, watched J.R. throw, watched a fastball register 100 mph, but instead of looking fresh and keen to deliver another one, Richard seemed a little wobbly to him. "He can't be hurt if he's throwing that hard," Cabell said. "He can't be hurt if his earned run average is 1.96. He can't be hurt if his record is 10–4."

Cabell felt that Richard was misunderstood, but that he was mercurial and sometimes inflamed that misunderstanding. "If you could talk to him, really get down with him, you could learn a whole lot about him. It's just that nobody ever tried. 'J' can be arrogant and he can be loving and he can be hateful and he can be mean. And the next minute, he can be happy and buying everybody food and laughing and everything."

Leading up to the All-Star Game, Richard wasn't even sure he would be able to compete. His arm felt dead and flat when he unleashed his speedy pitches. Three days after the game, while still in Los Angeles, Richard met with Dr. Frank Jobe, one of the most renowned sports medicine specialists in the United States. While J.R. did not obtain a clear diagnosis, he said that Jobe recommended he not pitch for 30 days. "I'm going fishing," Richard said.

Richard was apparently joking about that type of layoff and he decided to try a return to the mound on July 14 in a game against the Atlanta Braves. The Astros were in a pennant race and they needed him. Richard, a pitcher who hated to ever miss a start, felt that keenly. The game was played at the Astrodome, and Richard started. He pitched three and one-third innings, gave up one hit, and lowered his ERA to 1.90. But he had to leave the game abruptly. His vision was clouding, and he had difficulty reading catcher Luis Pujols' signs. The Braves won the game 2–0. Richard struck out Gary Matthews, Bob Horner, and Jeff Burroughs in order in the second inning.

J.R. did not want to come out for the fourth inning, and manager Bill Virdon urged him to keep trying. Virdon apparently did not truly believe that J.R. was injured. In the absence of hard medical proof, he was a doubter. After the game when sportswriters inquired about the reason for Richard's early departure, Astros team officials told them he had a stomachache. Two days later, on July 16 after Richard threw for about 20 minutes and complained of arm fatigue, Houston put J.R. on the 21-day disabled list. Pitching coach Mel Wright said, "J.R. was a deep mystery to me. I kept asking him, 'Do you feel any pain?' And he would reply, 'No pain.'"

J.R. was sent to Methodist Hospital for tests. Most of the tests were negative for neurological issues and the like, but a blockage—a blot clot—was found in Richard's right arm, the apparent root of his problems. The doctors concluded no surgery or special treatment was warranted at that time and told Richard he could resume light activities. Later, some other doctors insisted that the only thing Richard's exam turned up was a pinched nerve in his neck.

Professional athletes are supposed to play with pain. That is the warrior mentality they have been raised with, only reinforced by the attitude that they are supposed to give it all for the team's benefit regardless of health risk. Players and sportswriters looked at Richard's performance. They didn't see a bone sticking through his skin. There were whispers and gossip about how maybe Richard just didn't want to pitch, how he wasn't really ill or hurt. There were no ready answers for anyone.

Nolan Ryan, the new star addition to the pitching staff, was in his first year with the team and he admitted he did not know Richard very well. He did not feel comfortable crossing any invisible barriers to approach him for more information, figuring J.R. would talk if he wanted to, but Ryan still heard the gossip. "It wasn't just one person or one thing," Ryan said at the time. "It seemed that everything combined to feed the mystery: J.R's personality, the conflicting medical reports, the pressure of the pennant race. The more people talked about it, the more J.R. kept to himself."

Although others suggested it, owner John McMullen said he never believed Richard resented the presence of Ryan, who was being paid $1 million as a free agent to sign or about $150,000 more than Richard made. McMullen said he consulted with Richard before the Astros went after Ryan, so he couldn't have been surprised by the deal.

Any time Richard mentioned his subpar condition, people looked at him strangely. So he withdrew into himself more. "The strange thing was that you couldn't notice he was losing any of his stuff," Wright said. "His stuff was good, but he'd come into the dugout and say he didn't feel right, and you'd ask him what exactly was wrong, and he'd say, 'My arm is weak.' But then he would go for another inning maybe, and his stuff would still be good. I'm just a pitching coach, and the only way I can tell a guy isn't feeling good is that he doesn't have his stuff."

Once, Cabell was motioned over to the mound and was greeted by a distressed Richard. "He said, 'Man, I can't feel my fingers,'" Cabell said. "'I'm throwing 100 mph per hour and I can't feel the ball. I might kill someone.' I called for the manager, Bill Virdon. I don't think he and J.R. were the best of friends. We were in the pennant race, and it was his job to win the pennant. He said to J.R., 'Well, just see what you can do.' J.R. had a confident manner. He never missed a start. He was big and strong. And he was a free spirit. I just think people couldn't believe there could be anything wrong with this big, strong guy. Also, in the backs of the Astros' mind was the thought that if J.R. couldn't pitch, we wouldn't win the pennant."

On July 30, 1980, Richard was at the Astrodome doing a light workout with former Astros catcher Wilbur Howard when he collapsed on the field and was rushed to the hospital. This time the diagnosis was more frightening. The hospital spokesman characterized Richard's status this way: "His condition was unstable with some irregularities of the heart. It was apparent that he had suffered a stroke and that he had no pulse in his right carotid artery."

Richard underwent an immediate operation to relieve danger from the clot and, while most of his circulation was restored to normalcy when he awakened, he experienced weakness in his left arm and leg. A lead doctor on the case, Dr. Harold Brelsford, the Astros' team physician, said that the "original thrombosis" (the blood clot) discovered during J.R.'s tests was probably present for a couple of months and that it seemed appropriate at the time for him to be released from the hospital and allowed to resume light athletic activity. There were no answers, no explanations, he said, for why Richard's situation deteriorated so dramatically and thoroughly in the four days following the tests and for his collapse at the Astrodome. "I just don't know," Brelsford said. "His first clot was due to his pitching, but the second one we may never know why." Tom Reich, the agent for J.R., was furious at the way newspapers had portrayed Richard, essentially labeling him a faker. "In the name of God, how could you do this?" Reich said.

J.R. Richard

At the end of July and beginning of August, the Astros were on a long road trip out of town. They played in Philadelphia on July 30. I was inside the Astrodome doing a workout so I could be in some kind of shape when I came off the disabled list.

All of a sudden, I felt a high-pitched tone ringing in my left ear. And then I threw a couple of more pitches and became nauseated. A few minutes later, I threw a couple more pitches, then the feeling got so bad I was losing my equilibrium. I went down on the Astroturf. I had a headache, some confusion in my mind, and I felt weakness in my body. I didn't have knowledge of anything that was going on.

One official, who usually travels with the team, didn't go on the road. He was in the stadium looking down at me. I remember him coming over to me and saying, "J.R., are you all right? J.R., you all right?" I was lucky that someone was there who saw what happened.

He ran into the clubhouse and then back out and put a cold towel on my forehead. He kept asking me if I was all right and I think I said, "What do you think?" I was still conscious then.

I was lying on the floor of the Astrodome and I knew an ambulance was on its way. Before I passed out, I had all kinds of things running through my mind, but the chief one was, *What's wrong? What's wrong?* I couldn't even guess what had happened to me. In the years since, I've had a lot of people tell me they were at the game in the Astrodome when I fell down. There wasn't anybody there because the team was out of town. I basically missed the ride to the hospital. It's weird how people think they remember something like that. When they come up to me and say they were at the game I go, "Oh, you were at that game? *Really?*" I just let them go ahead and talk about it as if there had been a game. I don't know how they perceive that.

I heard an ambulance coming down the Astrodome ramp. I heard a car door. The ambulance came onto the field, and the medics picked me up and put me in the ambulance. I passed out. The next thing I knew I was at the hospital and I definitely was not all right. All that time I had been saying there was something wrong, and people didn't act like they believed me. Eventually, I learned that I had three strokes. When I went to the hospital I had a 24-carat gold chain around my neck. It was a religious chain. I never saw it again.

They did emergency surgery. I had a blood clot in my neck, on a blood vessel, I think. It was hard to understand, and I was woozy. The doctor told me that I was such a powerful pitcher that the muscles in my right shoulder had overdeveloped and were pressing against the ribs every time I threw. It caused an irritation, a blockage. I had a blockage 13 centimeters long. When they operated they took the blockage out of my arm—they almost cut my arm completely off—they cut into a rib and they took a vein from my stomach. They spliced two veins together in my arm and put a catheter in my stomach. The scar is right below my neck and near the shoulder blade. A blood clot had been lodged in my neck. It started cutting off the flow of blood to my brain.

To tell you the truth, at that point I wasn't even sure that everybody was sorry about what happened. People had been talking about how I was lazy. This meant they were wrong, and there was something wrong with me all of that time as I had been saying. I was taking every turn in the rotation. I was pitching as well as I ever had, so I don't know why anyone would accuse me of being lazy. Some people gossiped, trying to find reasons why I felt out of sorts. There were some people who spread the word that I was jealous of Nolan Ryan because he had a bigger contract. Nolan even said that he wondered if those rumors were bothering me and stressing me out. Some said that it was all psychological, that it was in my head. People say anything they want to say. I knew something was wrong. They kept saying that nothing was wrong. Deep down in my heart, I knew something was wrong. At that moment I was just about the best pitcher in baseball. Why wouldn't I want to pitch? It made no sense. It was illogical. But I knew something wasn't right. Why should I argue the point with them?

Even though I was putting up those great statistics, the one thing I was not doing was pitching as many complete games as I normally did. My arm would get fatigued and I could not stay in for nine innings. That wasn't me. I had made a career out of refusing to come out of games, out of pitching complete games. All of a sudden, I couldn't do it. The doctors explained why. I wasn't getting enough blood flow into my right arm. The circulation was off. I felt good in the All-Star Game and would like to have stayed in a little longer than two innings.

At that time sponsors were starting to see baseball players as celebrities and were thinking they could use players for marketing their products more. At the All-Star Game, people were throwing money at you and products. A shoe company said it would give you $5,000 to wear one of their shoes. I found $10,000 in my locker. I guess I was supposed to wear a pair. I was offered cash to wear a Nike glove. I was only going to pitch a couple of innings in my first All-Star Game so I didn't want to go out there with a new glove. I wasn't going to break in a new glove in two innings. I was afraid someone would hit a line drive back at me and I wouldn't be able to field it because I wasn't comfortable with my glove.

After the All-Star Game, I had a checkup in Los Angeles and then I had tests in Houston. What I have always wondered is how come if Houston is supposed to be one of the best medical centers in the world they couldn't treat me for a blood clot before I collapsed? Maybe you had to look for a blood clot to find a blood clot. But why send me home and not tell me to do anything for my health? Before that I saw Frank Jobe in California, and he couldn't find anything wrong either.

After the first examination by Jobe, I tried to pitch one more time, against the Atlanta Braves. But I had to come out of the game after a few innings. You know how I hated that. Then there was all of this talk, "What's wrong with him?" I just didn't have a clue what was wrong until I keeled over and had the surgery. At one point the doctors told me that the blood pressure in my left arm was normal, but it was zero in my right arm. That was because of the lack of circulation.

When I was in the hospital, the doctors took CAT scans and said I had suffered three separate strokes. Even after the surgery, I had a lot of problems on my left side. That included my arm and leg and the left side of my face. I had some blurred vision in my left eye. They used some medical terminology to describe everything, calling it "extensive arterial thoracic outlet syndrome." That means there can be pressure on the nerves, arteries, and blood vessels, and it can produce a blood clot or stroke. The impact on my pitching as I went along was that I could still start out strong for a few innings and then my arm started to ache and feel heavy. That's how they interpreted it in retrospect and that's what happened. That was before things got worse and I passed out.

I never could understand how the Astros handled things. If I meant so much to the ballclub and I started saying I had problems and didn't feel right, why didn't they send me to a doctor right away? I think teams are more sensitive to those situations now, especially with pitchers. They would automatically take you out of the game and make sure you went to the doctor the next day just to be on the safe side. That would be the first thing they would do. My friend, Enos Cabell, thought it was racial. He said something about African Americans always played with pain so they wouldn't lose their jobs. None of it made much sense, but that is a scenario. For a time I was looking for a good lawyer. I was ready to hire somebody. If I had hired an attorney, I would have told him, "Look at all this. Sue everybody." I would have walked away with $1 million.

You think that people care about you and your health and something like this happens, and it makes you wonder if they really do care all that much. In theory I was one of the most valuable assets the Astros had. I have no clue what they were thinking at all. During some of that time period, I thought the Astros just didn't give a damn about me.

After I was taken to the hospital and had the surgery and still had aftereffects of the stroke on my left side, some sportswriters wrote that it was a tragedy. No one could say right then, not the doctors or anyone else, if I would ever pitch for the Astros again. I had been worried for months and didn't understand what was happening to me. After I found out that I had something for real, and that it was not all in my head, that gave me a certain peace of mind. I mean, I didn't feel good. I was disappointed and upset and sick. But believe it or not, I didn't have any fear about anything. I was never afraid.

I always believed in God, my Father upstairs, so I didn't have any worries. I believed and felt God had my back. I said, "It is what it is." The reason I said that was the philosophy of "Why worry about something that you cannot control?" I know I am not in control of anything. We're just passing through this life. It wasn't my fault. I wasn't going to beat myself up. I was still alive. I thought that whatever it was that was wrong with me, even after the stroke, if I gave it enough time—I didn't care what it was—I would get better. What I hated hearing was that I wouldn't be able to pitch anymore. I felt awful about that. I wasn't convinced that was true, but I didn't like hearing it.

That made me feel terrible. I couldn't pitch anymore? I was depressed enough about what happened, but the idea that I couldn't pitch anymore depressed me even more. Even when

I got out of the hospital, I didn't want to do anything. I sat on my duff all day long. I was worried about the unknown, what was wrong with me. I didn't know anything about strokes. Who thinks about strokes when they are 30 years old and in top athletic shape? I was in top condition for my job as a pitcher. What could possibly go wrong? I was a big guy and weighed 240 pounds, but I had three percent body fat. I was strong and healthy. At that point in my career, I was probably the best pitcher in baseball. I thought I was invulnerable. I'm the only guy in the world who could throw a ball through a car wash and not get it wet.

Obviously, I had felt something was wrong for a long time, for weeks. But I certainly had no inkling that I was going to have a stroke. *A stroke?* You know before every season starts they were giving the players physicals. Let me ask you this question. If I was supposed to have a physical, what kind of a physical were they giving me? Why wouldn't my symptoms come up in a physical? Nothing is perfect, and I know guys have physicals and then go out and have a heart attack the next day, but it makes you wonder if it was a thorough physical. They told me the blood clot had been there for some time. It wasn't something that came on overnight.

You know how those sports physicals work. You go into the doctor's office, and they grab your balls and tell you to cough a couple of times. They say you're okay. They ask if you have any aches and pains, and you say you don't have any. They say you're okay. That's supposed to be your physical. It should be changed and improved. They should do all kinds of things to test you and check you out that take two or three days. They should check your arteries. They should give you an EKG. They should be more thorough.

For the most part, I wasn't sick. I didn't have a lot of symptoms that I could point to showing there was something major going wrong. What was wrong was inside me, and I didn't feel great. I didn't think there was something major going on. But there were clues that there was a problem. I had that numbness in my fingers. I kept getting spots, blood spots, at the end of a finger. They appeared like freckles. I kept telling people about the numbness. "This ain't right. Something ain't right. Things don't feel right." And I was told, "You're okay. Go pitch." I came up against that kind of attitude.

I was the one trying to figure out what the heck was wrong with me because it was out of the norm. All of a sudden, I didn't have the stamina to pitch a complete game. But I didn't want to walk away from anything. I wanted to get well and I wanted to pitch. I always figured I was going to pitch again.

2

Growing Up in Louisiana

J.R. Richard was a Louisiana kid. He was born March 7, 1950 in Vienna, Louisiana, a tiny town of several hundred people in the north central portion of the state. In the 2000 census, there were 424 residents. The one thing the community is famous for was being a place where Confederate troops trained during the Civil War in 1862. The community is located in Lincoln Parish. In Louisiana, unlike most states in the United States, counties are referred to as parishes. Vienna is located just north of Ruston, on the outskirts of that city of roughly 21,000 people. Ruston was Richard's orbit when he was growing up, and that is where he attended high school.

Ruston owes its creation to the coming of a railroad that was linking the Deep South to the West. The community was founded in 1883. Louisiana Tech, with a student population of more than 11,000, is located in Ruston, and the growing university has helped gain attention for the city over the years whenever its sports teams have been successful. This was notably true when future Hall of Fame basketball player Karl Malone was competing for the Bulldogs. The 6'9", 250-pound basketball star played for Louisiana Tech between 1982 and 1985. For several years the school was also renowned for its women's basketball teams.

Situated just six miles to the west of Ruston is Grambling University, where throughout Richard's youth the football team was coached by the legendary Eddie Robinson. Robinson, who actually passed away in Ruston in 2007 at age 88, coached Grambling for 56 years and won 408 football games. The historically black college and its sports teams were an inspiration to young Richard and other African American families in Ruston. Among those who thrived in Ruston's sports-rich environment besides J.R. Richard were future Major League Baseball star Ralph Garr and football Hall of Famer Fred Dean.

Richard attended now-defunct Lincoln High School, where he became an all-around athlete, but in his younger days, growing up in the 1950s and 1960s, he was like all his other friends, playing ball on a nearby field or in the gym and competing in football, basketball, or baseball, depending on the season.

J.R. Richard

Vienna was so small that all it had was one caution light. At the time I think there were around 500 people living there. I grew up in a house that was part of a village almost. There were eight people in my family. My father was James Clayton Richard. My mother was named Elizabeth Richard. Her maiden name was Frost. My older brother had the same name as my father. He was about six years older than me. My brother Lamar was right behind me, and then Thomas was right behind him. My sister Pam was next in line, and my youngest brother was

Dexter. He died of kidney failure. That was a sad situation. He was in his 20s and he just got tired of all of the treatments and spending so much time in the hospital and just let go. He stopped getting dialysis and let things just happen. There were five boys and one girl, though Pam did everything the boys would do. She wanted to play ball with us, too. We had a lot of James' in one house, so I became J.R.

My dad was a lumber grader. He stood in position and he judged the quality of the lumber cut. He decided what quality the lumber was and how it was sorted into piles for building materials. It was, "You go here. You go there." From the time I was a small boy, my father had a sawmill. I remember shoveling sawdust.

My mother was a cook at my elementary school at the same time I was going there. She gave me lectures on how to eat right. The school was called Union Village, and it was in a town called Dubach. Fred Dean, who was a defensive end, and I, are about the same age. He still has a home in Ruston. He's a preacher in Louisiana.

When I was a little kid, I liked to be outdoors. As a child I would go out and gather up a pocket full of rocks, then go into the woods, and take target practice. I threw at birds or rabbits, whatever I could throw at. That's one way I developed my arm. I killed quite a few of them. I didn't really do it to get food for my family. I think that throwing the rocks was a major thing that contributed to me building strength in my arm and my right shoulder. As you build strength, you build speed. That translated to baseball, though some of it came naturally.

Like something out of the movie *Forrest Gump*, I was running all of the time. If someone made a movie about my life, the youngster in the movie would be throwing all of the time the way Forrest Gump was running all of the time. When I was a kid, I ran everywhere I went. I ran more as a kid than I did as a pitcher. Kids have so much energy. But they always say the old, gray mare ain't what she used to be. I don't think my knees would like it if I ran that much now. My spine wouldn't like it either.

Generally, we ate some of the rabbits we killed. By then I had a BB gun and I used to shoot rabbits with that and we cooked those. I was a fantastic shot with the BB gun. I used to go hunting with my uncle, my cousin, my brother, and my uncle's son. I'd go over to my uncle's house, and we went hunting from there. We killed birds and then built fires in the woods, roasted them, and ate them. I loved the outdoors. I still love to go fishing. We fished for anything we could catch. We didn't stay in the woods overnight much. We didn't camp often. Mostly all we did was go out for the day.

We used to run through the woods and climb trees. We picked Muscadine grapes and gathered food from pear trees, pecan trees, and hickory nut trees. I ate all of that stuff as well as the rabbits. Just like any other kids, if we got bored, we found some mischief. For some strange reason, one of my brothers and I decided we wanted to cut down a sweet gum tree on the top of the hill where we played a lot. I got the idea we could tie a rope to the top of the sweet gum tree, and when we cut it down, we could make it fall over. There was no reason for it. We were bored. I got a real beatdown for that one. Another time we were bored and started throwing rocks at gas trucks. We hit a truck one time, and the man stopped and got out. We started running as soon as we saw the brake lights. We shot right home, and when he drove up, we were playing in the house like there was nothing going on. We were the only house out there, though, so he knew where to go.

It took me a little while, but I learned to stay out of trouble and keep my nose clean. I found out which kids not to run with. If you know right from wrong, you don't have an excuse. You have to find out who you are. Most kids don't know who they are, and they get in trouble following others. A lot of basically good kids get led astray. They are hanging out with the wrong guy. But if you did something wrong in our house, there was no bargaining with my dad. He told us one time, and if you broke the rules, you got a whupping. We didn't get spankings. We got beatings.

The Bible talks about respecting your father and the father showing love for his children by punishing them when they did wrong. When I was that age, I probably wish that passage had been left out, but I don't feel that way today. If you do something wrong and you get punished for it, it helps you grow up to be a better man.

After my father got his sawmill going, we used to sneak in there and take out oblong wooden blocks, put a nail in them, get a hanger from what we hung our clothes on and used spools of thread and called them logging trucks. We made some of our own toys. We made bows and arrows. We created arrows from bushes and weeds. To make them stiff, we rubbed them down with tar we took from the middle of the road. We used a stick pin for the tip and we shot the arrows and killed birds.

These were not very powerful bows and arrows. They were nothing like those compound bows they use now. When we hunted raccoons, we used .22 rifles. They were good for hunting deer, too. If you shoot a deer in the neck, it's a done deal. A spine hit means he ain't going nowhere. If you hit a deer in the rump, you might have to chase him for a while, like five or six miles. My daddy gave us one shell for the .22. With that gun shell, you had better bring something back. The worst thing that could happen was that you had to shoot a snake. You had to bring it back home.

My older brother, James, used to play softball for a county team. He was older so he got involved in sports before I did. When I was about 12 or 13, I started playing softball with a distant relative of mine named John who was also a friend. He would come over and spend the summer with us one year, and I would go spend the summer with him the next year. When I went to his house one year, they were just getting ready to start the softball season in that area. They referred to it as "organized" softball. I thought, *What in the world is "organized?"*

I was a country boy, and we played on our own. There were no teams with uniforms and sponsors and that stuff. Well, since I was with John that summer, I went everywhere he went. So I started playing. I was big for my age but still smaller than the other kids because I was younger than they were. What started out as softball led me to baseball. I had grown up in the country where I was born, but then we moved into Ruston, a bigger city. Then the opportunities turned into baseball. I wanted to make new friends because I was new to the community and I started playing sandlot baseball. I had a friend there named Robert Carr who was a pitcher so I became a pitcher.

At this field the mound was a rubber tire that was mostly buried in the ground. We didn't have any benches, so we had to stand up the whole game when we weren't out in the field.

This was not a fenced-in park. The outfield ended where the woods started. If you hit a ball into the woods, it was a home run. It was like in that movie *Field of Dreams* where they hit the ball into the cornfield, and it kind of disappeared. For us it wasn't that the ball got lost, but if it went into the woods it was going to be a home run and not just because of the distance. By the time anybody picked up the ball, the batter was going to be running home anyway.

I was growing fast and was the tallest guy around. We were not financially well off, so some of my clothes were handed down. It was hard to buy new ones, too, because I grew too fast. My pants used to be really short. I was taller than anyone else in the family. I inherited my size from my grandfather on my mother's side. He was a huge man. As a matter of fact, he was a log hauler. He used to work in the woods and haul logs with a mule up the road. They deposited the logs in one place to be ready when the truck came by and picked up the pile. That's what he did for a living. A lot of the animals were big old horses, like the Clydesdales or draft horses, but we called them log mules. They might have been 18 hands high.

Also when I was pretty young, there was a guy in the area named Buck Houston. His eyes were always bloodshot because he drank, but he packed us kids up in a raggedy pickup truck and took us around to play baseball in different places, to other towns maybe an hour away. We'd get to our destination, jump out of the truck, get some bats, and go out there on a field and play. We didn't have any idea of it being called "organized" baseball.

I think my first glove was a softball glove. It was mediocre at best. It was not genuine leather. It was some leather-like substance that was called "pleather." It's fake leather. It's shinier than real leather and cheaper. It reminded me more of plastic. I had a Jackie Robinson bat with a big handle. I just fell in love with it playing softball because the handle was so big and I had big hands. It's the only bat I really felt comfortable with.

The trees made up the border of the outfield, and there were railroad tracks even farther away. I hit some home runs behind the trees. If you hit the railroad tracks, my, that was a ding-dong. That meant the ball was really traveling. You had to hit the trees first.

My mother did not want us kids around the house underfoot in the summer when we were out of school. She would say, "You've got no business in this house. You need to move. Go out and play. If you're lazy, come in the house and go to sleep."

Sandlot ball helped me when I was starting out. There was a catcher whose name was Haywood, and he would preach the entire game. He kept talking the whole game. When I wound up, he was talking. When I threw a pitch, he was talking. He never stopped talking. It was about anything and everything. A lot of times, it was just basic conversation. He talked to every hitter when he stepped into the batter's box. Some catchers in the majors talked to hitters, too, as a way to distract them.

I first started playing baseball on playgrounds and only after that became involved with organized teams. I take that to mean that God has a plan for your life. He is always pushing you to certain places where you should go. You don't know you need to be there, but he does. Baseball was where I was supposed to go.

Around that time of my life, I began attending Grambling Junior High and I was teased a lot because my clothes didn't fit. They were my "short pants." I didn't care for that situation very much. I decided I wanted a change. It seemed most of the students were teacher's kids. My friend Robert went to a different school in Ruston and I decided that's where I wanted to go. I used to run about a mile every morning to catch the bus for school and I caught it with Robert and his brother Joseph.

When I was junior high aged, I liked baseball, but I wasn't very good yet. I did not play on a team in junior high. I did not play until I got to Lincoln High School. It was a four-year high school, so it started with ninth grade.

About this time my father started a sawmill for extra income. He made broom handles on the weekends. I spent time with him, and we became closer then. He used to counsel me, and one thing he said often was, "Son, have more time for your kids than I have had for you." That resonated with me, and I thought he was saying that I should try to be the best I could possibly be, to be a success so I didn't have to work as hard as he. He motivated me. That stuck to me like glue. I just wanted to be the best I could at everything. Everything included shooting marbles, spitting across the street, anything. Any time there was a game or a contest of any kind I would be a competitor, a die-hard competitor.

By the time I got to high school, I had fallen in love with sports. I just loved sports. I played football, basketball, and baseball. They were pretty much all of the sports we had. I was good at everything. By the time I finished high school, I had grown into my man-sized height. I was 6'8" and weighed 220 pounds and kept growing to 240 pounds.

My father was never an athlete. I don't even know if he liked sports; he never said. He was rooting for me, but he never went to games. He never went to a game when I was in high school, but much later when I was playing with the Houston Astros, I had it in my contract that he could come to Houston, all expenses paid, to see a game. But that was years later in my career.

I first started playing football when I entered high school in the fall of 1966. I was a little rough around the edges. I made the team, but I definitely wasn't a star. When I first started, I played guard or tackle because I was so big. They threw me out there on the defensive line and said, "You stop them." It was like that at first. My first position was defensive end. Sometimes on short yardage, I was put in to run and try to pick up a first down. I played everything at first, except center.

They didn't have the same rules about eligibility when I was in high school. There were some older guys still in the school that were not of the traditional age for high school, but they were still enrolled and they played football. I had my knocks and bruises and bloody lips and everything in football. I always made sure to fix up everything before I got home so my mother wouldn't notice, or at least if she noticed, she wouldn't think it was a big issue and make me stop playing.

I stuck with it. I wasn't going to quit just because it got a little bit rough. I stayed with it, and by my junior year, I became quarterback of the team because of my strong arm. I went from a lineman to a backfield player, and that included defense. The quarterback played safety, too. I was pretty quick and I was kind of a utility man. Wherever they needed me, I went there. Playing defense was interesting. As a safety I did a lot of blitzing. I just enjoyed the game, especially the competitiveness. The Lincoln High Bears were a pretty good football team. We went undefeated one year. We won a state championship my junior year.

This was not a big high school. We only had over a hundred students or so, but we did pretty well. I went from football to basketball to baseball through the seasons. By the time I was a junior, I was a prominent player in all three sports. For someone who was not a particularly good athlete in junior high school this was a big jump in confidence. It felt good.

I really became a star high school athlete. By the time I finished playing in high school, I had so many scholarship offers from different colleges. I couldn't tell you how many. I heard from hundreds of schools. Some wanted me to play football. Some wanted me to play basketball. And then there was baseball.

3

Becoming a Pitcher

When it came to sports, J.R. Richard was a phenom across the spectrum of football, basketball, and baseball at Lincoln High School. He became the football team's quarterback as a junior after dabbling at just about every other position. J.R. was built for basketball and he could score and rebound in close, but he was also a passing whiz. He saw the court with great vision. Looking back he believes that if he had gone to college on a basketball scholarship he would have morphed into a Magic Johnson-type oversized point guard. They are about the same height, and Richard envisioned a professional team perhaps seeing his potential as a big man handling the ball on the fly the way that Magic did. "He was an all-around athlete. If you can catch a football, you can catch a baseball," said his high school football coach, Robert Smith. "He was able to throw a football and a baseball and he is a big man. I believe if he had played any sport he would have been considered one of the greatest. I think he would have set many records if he stayed healthy."

In baseball, Richard was such a dominating pitcher that the Bears were lucky if other school teams on the schedule showed up when J.R. was due to pitch. He pitched no-hitters on demand almost, blanking foes and shutting them down routinely. By the time Richard graduated from high school in 1969, he was probably the best known schoolboy athlete in Louisiana, and college recruiters from all over the nation and baseball scouts from major league teams all knew his name.

Richard's main mentor when he was in high school was Robert Smith, and the two men remain close today. Smith still lives in Ruston, and J.R. visits him when he returns to Ruston from Houston to see family. The two cities are about five hours apart by road. Coaching football, basketball, and baseball at Lincoln for 10 years, Smith was a multi-faceted leader of boys. After integration in 1970, when high schools in Ruston merged, he spent 10 more years as an assistant coach at Ruston High and then became head coach there. The old Lincoln High School building serves as a junior high school now.

A sturdily built man of 80, Smith lives in a pleasant home not far from the old school, though in Ruston nothing is very far apart. One day while driving through town, J.R. said, "You have to be an idiot to get lost" in the community. Then he promptly made a wrong turn because he hadn't been back in that neighborhood for a while. J.R. laughed at his own accidental joke. Of course, it only took driving one more block to correct the driving error.

Smith has short, white hair and a salt and pepper mustache. On a sultry summer afternoon he was wearing a short-sleeved, buttoned-down-the-front shirt. "The first time I saw J.R. he was on a baseball field," Smith said, noting that Richard was playing with his friend

Robert Carr. "I saw a big, old, tall kid who was just striking everyone out." I talked to him and said, "I need you at Lincoln High School.'"

Richard was terrific from the start in baseball, the way Smith remembers it. "When he first came to us, we went 27–0 and won the state championship in baseball," Smith said. "He had everything it took at that time. He had everything in duplicate. He trained well and he listened to me. Every day those pitchers ran. Louisiana Tech had never had a black baseball player, but they would have signed J.R."

Richard was besieged by mail from college coaches, some of them football coaches and some of them basketball. Baseball offered a different path to the top. He would not have to attend school for four more years and he could begin getting paid right after high school graduation. "It was stated in his signing with the Astros that they would pay for his college education," Smith said. "If he didn't make it with the team, they would pay for his college."

Richard, of course, did make it big with the Astros, though he did also attend Arizona State for a while. Ralph Garr was one notable baseball player who observed a young J.R. playing in high school and then later in the majors. Garr was born in nearby Monroe, Louisiana, also attended Ruston High, and played for Grambling State before becoming a professional player. He spent 13 years in the majors between 1968 and 1980.

Even though Garr is almost five years older than Richard, he saw him pitch some high school games and he said it was no contest between the thrower and any of the locals who tried to hit him. "I signed out of Grambling, and he signed out of high school at about the same time," Garr said. "When he pitched against the high school kids, they had no chance at all against him. He was very intelligent and he had everything going for him. They talk about these guys throwing now and how fast they are, but they weren't throwing harder than J.R."

J.R. Richard

When I was in high school, I enjoyed basketball more than I did baseball. I considered myself a better basketball player than baseball player. Basketball seemed like more of a challenge. We had to play together, but it still seemed like an individual sport. I looked at myself as being the best, but if not for the team assisting me on my shots, I couldn't have been what I was without them. I couldn't play five guys by myself.

As a kid I played everything. Sports have changed. Now kids start to specialize at really young ages. They are only a baseball player or a football player. It's a shame. You may want to develop different skills playing one sport, and skills may transfer from one to the other. If you play several sports, you are developing all things. I went from football to basketball to baseball. My first year of high school baseball I pitched and then I played left field when I wasn't on the mound. I had that game where I hit four home runs off of four different pitchers and recorded 10 runs batted in. I was a pretty good hitter.

We beat Jackson High of Jonesboro 48–0 so they kept changing pitchers. We scored 15 runs in the fourth inning and we sent someone over to the other coach and said, "This is a blowout. Do you want to quit?" And the coach said no. We just kept pouring it on, pouring it on. It was only a seven-inning game. I enjoyed myself that day.

After trying all of those positions in football I really started to develop. Coach Smith saw me throw a football 75 yards. I was just starting to come into my own. I had that attitude in me about being the best at anything I did. One thing I did the best in high school was break up fights. I was bigger than everyone else, and no one wanted to fight with me. But I was a peacemaker. That was just my attitude. I didn't want anyone to challenge me, and no one wanted to do that. I wasn't about fighting. I always figured there could be a peaceful solution. Somebody had to think clearly and step in who wasn't mad.

My friend, Robert Carr, got me started in pitching and he encouraged me to go to Lincoln High School. He pitched, too. Coach Robert Smith also had encouraging words for me from the first time I came to Lincoln. The teasing at Grambling Junior High bothered me. I didn't need extra stress. I went to Lincoln so I wouldn't get ribbed or teased. When we played against Grambling High School, I got revenge in all three sports. We played them all of the time.

Coach Smith was a big influence on me. He was a real motivator. He said things like, "I can only coach you so much. I can tell you how to do this, but the ultimate decision on how you do something is yours. You can be as good as you want. You can be less than your potential if you want. But the ultimate choice is up to you. You can be what you want to be. I've given you the tools to work with."

One thing Coach Smith did emphasize was discipline. I closely watched the way he interacted with other kids. I learned to love other people from him. He took other kids who weren't so fortunate and didn't have the money for basic things and bought them food or clothes. They might be guys on the football or basketball teams who didn't have much because their mothers couldn't afford it.

Coach Smith's relationship with us went beyond the field. I tried to follow his example later on when I was in baseball and I made a good paycheck. I gave people a lot of things. When I was in big cities, I saw homeless people on the street. I would ask, "When was the last time you ate?" I didn't give them money because I knew many of them would spend it on booze. I told them I would get them something to eat. Too many of those homeless guys were alcoholics, and you knew what was going to happen if you gave them money.

From studying the Bible, I learned that if you take them out to eat or give them money, the blessing is on you. You have done your job to help by giving them money. If they want to piss it away, let them piss it away. But I knew after they got through being drunk, they were still going to wake up hungry.

When you are young and you have a coach you respect and who you know wants to help you, that's a good thing. But sometimes you are too immature to recognize everything he is telling you. He can help you in the moment, but sometimes you hear his voice later in life and then understand the message he was trying to get across to you when you were a teenager. You become older and wiser. You understand more about what he was trying to say back then when you were busy being foolish. The advice helps you grow up and become what you should be. Right now I love to give back to kids, and part of that reason was the example set for me by Coach Smith. I try to give to kids who don't have the same opportunities that I had. I want to give back to them.

I didn't have any other local role models who I followed and I didn't follow Major League Baseball very closely. I didn't get to any games. We didn't have a TV, and if you don't have a TV, you can't watch it. But my one baseball idol was Bob Gibson, the St. Louis Cardinals pitcher. The Cardinals won the 1967 World Series in seven games against the Boston Red Sox, and Bob Gibson was the Most Valuable Player. I listened to it on the radio and I imagined being like Bob Gibson. He won three games, and all of them were complete games. He was a fastball pitcher and he was my favorite player.

In the beginning when I pitched a game in school my thing was to just be the best you could every time out. You're pitching the best you possibly can. I didn't know what numbers I had, but I learned that I was a good pitcher. I threw fast, but I had to learn to pitch. That meant that I had to understand when it was the best time not to throw as fast as I could, but to mix in change-ups, off-speed pitches to go with my speed. Early on I could have been more devastating. I didn't have all of the actions of a great pitcher. I didn't have much off-speed stuff. That was true in high school, and I was still learning that in the major leagues.

There is no question that when I was in high school speed was the No. 1 thing. For that matter it was in the pros, too. All scouts are looking for speed right now. Hitters couldn't catch up to my fastball, and that was my advantage. In the beginning it was just winding up and throwing it.

One of the strangest things that happened to me with regard to pitching occurred on a day when I was home in Louisiana just sitting on the front porch. It was extremely hot, and there was nothing to do. I decided to take a walk. Along the side of the road near my house, I found a book about pitching. It was along Highway 167. It was just lying there as if it was waiting for me, as if God himself had put it there just for me. It was called *How To Pitch*. My fastball came naturally, but from studying this book, I learned how to throw the slider. It had instruction about the knuckleball, too, but all I was concerned about was the slider. I wish I still had that book, but I don't know where it went.

At that time of my life, I wasn't doing much reading, but I remember going through that book studying every page. I looked at the rotation of your arm when you throw and I went outside and followed the instructions by throwing rocks. They had pictures in the book about the placement of your fingers when you tried to throw a certain kind of pitch. I really learned how to throw. I was kind of self-taught.

I got better. Everything improved. Improvement comes from knowledge of the game. It's not all about being a good athlete. There's knowledge of football, knowledge of basketball, knowledge of baseball. This book helped me get knowledge of baseball. I still had the same mentality about being competitive.

Once my father talked to me about being the best at what I did. I never let that thought go. I tried to instill that same thinking in my kids. I still have that philosophy today. When I was young mostly, I just reared back and threw my fastball as hard as I could. I enjoyed that. It was fun because I was dominating. It's always fun when you win and hitters can't hit you. I was very fast, so I didn't have to throw at people to back them off the plate in the batter's box. They did it on their own.

One time, when I was pitching in Oklahoma City, I did throw at somebody. The guy stood right up close on the plate, and he kind of dared you to throw inside. Another pitcher, Scipio Spinks, a major leaguer who was a friend of mine, hit him, but the guy still stood close to the plate. Later, when I was pitching I was thinking of throwing at him, but really what happened was that one pitch got away from me and hit him in the head. The pitch shattered his helmet. They took him out on a stretcher, and I haven't seen him since. I think he quit playing baseball. He was lucky to be alive.

I never lost a game pitching in high school. I finished my senior year 11–0, and my earned run average was 0.00. I was a strikeout guy. The Bears were a really good team, and I started to get noticed. I can't actually remember the first recruiting letter I got, but coaches started writing to me. Then the sportswriter Heywood Hale Broun came to town. He said he had heard about me. He was so famous that when he wrote something it went worldwide. He came from New York to see me.

In Ruston we had a diamond at a place called Fraser Field. It had wire fencing around it, and I threw a pitch that went right through the chicken wire. There were a lot of scouts in the stands when that happened. Nobody had done that. I scattered the chickens, so to speak.

When my senior season ended, a whole bunch of scouts came to Ruston to work me out before the amateur draft. I was lucky that my arm never hurt. We had finished the season and finished the playoffs, and they all wanted me to throw for them. I never had arm fatigue and for that reason I could deliver everything with perfection. I know lots of guys have their arms give out, but I'm only speaking for myself, and I never had arm problems.

I did get a lot of attention in high school, but I don't think it changed me. It seemed to me that in a small high school everybody just kind of paid attention to themselves. I didn't present myself as being bigger or better than anybody else. I went about my normal day at school and at baseball practice. I didn't run around saying, "I'm on TV," or this, that, or the other. I didn't do any of that because I wasn't raised like that.

Yes, I got the attention for being a good athlete, but I didn't think anything about it. Even after being a pitcher in the big leagues for the Houston Astros, I just think I'm a regular guy but a guy who had a different job. I bleed the same blood as everybody else. I cry the same tears as everybody else. Of course, I jump both legs at a time when I put my pants on. Just kidding. I put my pants on one leg at a time like everybody else.

It was nice that all of these colleges and teams were interested in me and offering scholarships, but I didn't think much about it. I stuck to my philosophy of training to be the best at whatever I tried and figured it would all work out.

In football I completed 65 percent of my passes, and that was a long time before the NFL started emphasizing passing percentage the way it does now. I also averaged 48 yards per punt. During the basketball season as a senior, I averaged 35 points a game and 22 rebounds. That's why I thought I was a better basketball player. One of my basketball heroes was Willis Reed, who won world championships with the New York Knicks. But before that he played for Grambling, and I was a big fan. Willis Reed was why I thought I might try to play basketball for the Tigers. In baseball my senior year I struck out 89 hitters in 43 innings and batted .378.

I liked football, basketball, and baseball, but at the end of high school, I chose baseball for my career. It was about the signing bonus. I had a friend who had played for Grambling High, and he was a pitcher in Chicago. I thought, *Man, this guy went to the pros from high school. He must be some kind of good.* I didn't really think I had the ability to do that. See, I had always been taught from the Bible not to boast about what you do. Let your actions speak for themselves and let other people talk about how good you are. I have always had that attitude and I have tried to keep that attitude.

Pretty much all of the teams were interested in me. The Astros made me their No. 1 draft pick in 1969. Sometimes I wish I had gone to the New York Yankees because I might have four or five championship rings. But you can't control the team that drafts you. At first I was turned off by the Astros because when the scout came to my house to talk about joining the team I could smell alcohol on his breath. Sometimes I got in my car and left, thinking, *I ain't got time to deal with that.*

After I was drafted by the Astros, the team sent someone to the house to sign me. I was just a dumb country boy, and back then they didn't pay that much money, but I got a six-figure bonus. That was a one-time thing, not a salary. Compare that to the money now. Heck, even by 1977 I was only making $75,000 a year. I was naïve. I hadn't been anywhere. We weren't exactly sharecroppers, but we raised our own food, hunted rabbits, hunted for deer and other meat. We did everything we could to obtain our own food directly. My mom could can vegetables and preserves. We did everything we could for ourselves. It's a good lifestyle.

It's an inexpensive lifestyle, too, but a good one because all of the food you eat is natural food. It doesn't have preservatives, synthetics, or chemicals in it. That's what killing a lot of people today. When you cook some foods, it kills the nutrition, the minerals, and vitamins. So you're really eating dead food. Too much of anything isn't good for you. It was a different age of communication, too. I actually found out I was drafted by the Astros when a local guy who was an attorney came to the house. He wanted to be my lawyer and represent me. I didn't know anything about being drafted or how much money was the right amount.

The money is very different and much bigger in baseball now, but the offer was for more money than I had ever seen in my life. Since I was a No. 1 draft pick, they were paying pretty good money. That was kind of an exception to the rule at the time, and it was a very pleasant surprise to me.

The one thing I had always wanted and couldn't afford was my own car. I took some of the bonus money and bought my first car. It was a 1969 Plymouth GTX. I'd had my eye on it for a while. That's what I wanted. I was 19 years old and I was leaving home—off to become a professional baseball player.

4

The Minor Leagues

Once he cut his deal with the Houston Astros, J.R. Richard was off to make good as a professional baseball player. His first assignment was in Mesa, Arizona, in the Arizona Instructional League. Richard discovered quite quickly that professional players were more than a notch above the Louisiana high school players. His brief stay among other rookies produced a 1–3 record with a 4.33 ERA.

It had been a long time since Richard had experienced such difficulties on a baseball mound. But his stay in Arizona was short. The Astros shifted J.R. to the Covington, Virginia, team in the Appalachian League, another low-level minor league outfit. He finished 5–4, and while he struck out 71 batters in 56 innings, Richard was also dinged for quite a few runs. At that point in Richard's young career, he threw fast but was somewhat wild. He had not completely mastered his control. A super fast pitcher with iffy control scares the heck out of batters. He may not even be trying to intimidate them, but if he doesn't have mastery over the high, hard one, then not even he can predict where the throw will end up. On the plus side, that does not breed confidence in batters and can mess with their concentration. They have trouble connecting with the ball if they are frightened for their health.

Going straight from high school to the minors, Richard was making a big jump, and it was a given that—with his finite experience and small number of innings—it was going to take a little while to leap to the majors. Covington, Virginia, which is not to be confused with the Covington, Kentucky, that is located just across the state line from Cincinnati, Ohio, was not his favorite place.

J.R. Richard

They had huge rattlesnakes up there in Covington. Luckily, I didn't see any on the field during a game. Just getting there in the mountains left me feeling queasy. I flew in on the old Piedmont Airlines, and it wasn't so much that the plane ride made me sick. It was the cab ride afterward coming down the mountains. That made me sick.

It was exciting to sign a contract with the Astros. We did the paperwork in my home. My father and mother were both there. They were happy for me, but I don't think they really understood the magnitude of the signing of a professional contract. They gave me a good bonus contract, but I knew it didn't guarantee anything. Every step of the way in baseball it gets harder, and there are always more good guys you play against at each level. My thinking was that I just wanted to play and to win games. I wasn't thinking about anything special for me. I just wanted to play and I wanted to keep that attitude my father instilled in me.

I knew I had been a dominating pitcher in high school in Ruston, Louisiana, but I also knew that they weren't going to care much about that in Covington, Virginia. I dominated, and that said a lot about me, but going into the pros was literally a different ball game. I tried not to have any expectations at all. I was a young guy just starting out and I suppose I was a little bit naïve about life. I hadn't been anywhere. I tried to focus all of my energy on playing, on pitching.

My confidence was good. I had seen good results. Out West in the Instructional League my rookie year, I was as wild as the Wild West in Texas. I walked everybody in the ballpark my first game, including the concession stand workers. It was almost like Ricky "Wild Thing" Vaughn, the pitcher Charlie Sheen played in *Major League*. That was me.

When I got taken out of the game because I couldn't get the ball over the plate, I remember starting to cry on my way to the clubhouse. That was not me on the mound, and I made a resolution that I never wanted that to happen to me again. Every day I talked to the manager and the coaches about what I could do to improve myself. They told me I needed to run more so I increased my running exponentially. I ran around the ballpark quite a bit.

I was startled when I went out for that first game and was so wild. I hadn't been wild in high school. I didn't think I was nervous. To be honest, I don't know why that happened. I didn't have a clue. I was just throwing the ball. I couldn't explain it. If I was nervous, that would have been a reason, but I never did think about being nervous when they put me in.

The Appalachian League was a rookie league. We didn't play a full season like the majors and we finished with a 31–36 record. The manager was Dick Bogard. There were some other young guys on that team that were just starting out, too, and made it to the majors. You have to understand that only a small percentage of players in rookie league play, go on, and move up through the minor league chain and ever play a game in the majors. But we had some good guys who did make it.

One of those players was Mike Easler, a pretty good hitter. Stan Papi played some in the majors. Pat Darcy was a pitcher and like me he was only 19 at the time. Darcy played for the Reds. He had one good year when he went 11–5, but his career was over early.

My manager was very helpful and very encouraging, even when I was adapting to better hitters than I had seen in high school, and things were not going so well. He would say, "You are going to be in the major leagues within a year." He kept on instilling positive things in me. Even when I was doing wrong, he was always positive, teaching me. He didn't want me to get down on myself. He saw potential in me. When I gave up so many runs after pitching so many shutouts in high school, it was easy for me to get down on myself, but he just wouldn't let me. He kept on saying, "You're going to the major leagues. You're going to the major leagues." When you are that young and you are away from home for the first time, it's hard to look very far ahead.

My first year in the minors as a young guy, I did pitch like a young guy. I wasn't used to losing games, but it didn't bother me as much as it might have. I knew that in the pros no one is perfect. Nobody wins every game. I was giving up more runs than I was used to giving up, too, but I managed to not let it bother me. I kept my concentration and my focus on improving. My manager always acted as if he believed in me, and that was a great help.

One of the interesting things was being away from home for the first time. In rookie league ball, the players are all 19 and 20, so your teammates are the same age you are. You don't feel that disparity yet when you move up to Single or Double A and there are veterans who have been around baseball for years.

My roommate that year in rookie ball was Easler, who later played for the Pittsburgh Pirates. Mike played 14 years in the majors and he batted .293. He was a good hitter, and his nickname was "Hit Man." We lived in the same house together, but we never went out to do anything. We just played ball. We never went out on the town. We were both Christians and still are. All we thought about doing was advancing to a higher level of the minors and making it to the majors.

I was raised as a church-goer. That was the environment for me in Ruston. My father made the kids go to church, but he stayed at home. He didn't care what you did on a Saturday night or how late you stayed out. You had to get up to go to church. If you got home at 7:00 AM, and church was at 8:00 AM, you had better go to church or you were going to get a beatdown. We went to church on a consistent basis, even if my father didn't, and church made a big impact on my life. The Bible says, "raise up a child, which way he should go, you raise up a child leaning and depending on God." It suggested that if a child was exposed to church that, even if he left religion, he would always come back to it because those were his roots. It's just like salmon. Fish that are born in one place go off into the ocean, but they always migrate back to where they were born to spawn. Religion was an important part of my life when I was a kid, and I strayed away from the ministry, but I am back and I am back with a vengeance, and things are a lot better in my life for it. I have more sense in my 60s than I did when I was younger and when I did things just off the cuff.

There were definitely a lot of hills around Covington. There are hills everywhere. We rode buses up and down all of those hills. We reached a town for an away game once, and when we got there, the field was under three feet of water. There was nothing we could do but just turn around and go home. It was, "Enjoy your day off."

Being so far from home for the first time and not being around my parents and siblings, I was homesick. I coped with it pretty much one day at a time. I tried not to dwell on it too much. Once I was there with the team for a while, I got adjusted to the place. I had lived a country lifestyle. We never did do much going out at home in Louisiana either. We never went much of anywhere as a family except to my grandfather's all of the time for the weekend. We would go to my grandparents' house and eat and visit. Outside of that we didn't visit many people. So I was kind of used to staying at home and not doing anything. I wasn't a bright lights, big city guy by any means. That wasn't in my upbringing.

When you play in the minors, you pretty much play baseball every day. They don't schedule many off days, especially in those short-season leagues. You show up for the team and you play a game almost every day. After being so wild at first, I felt myself getting better. In some of the later games when I pitched, I didn't walk as many guys. I felt as if I was getting smarter and better about pitching to better hitters right up through the end of the year.

And I actually batted .261. I didn't play that much, but even though I didn't hit a home run, I did knock in six runs.

That was before the designated hitter was introduced, and pitchers batted all of the time in the minors, not just in the National League.

As a pitcher I struck out a lot of guys, but my earned run average (6.59) stunk. My delivery was off, and that's why my control was so bad. I learned that no matter what a hitter did against me I had to have immediate amnesia. I couldn't afford to let what he did affect how I pitched to the next batter. So I was never concerned about him again. I just always wanted to focus on the next guy coming up.

One thing that was different was having men on base against me often. In high school I practically never had guys on base. When it first happened for Covington, I forgot about it. Instead of pitching from a stretch to hold the runner on, I pitched from a full windup. That was one thing I pretty much had to learn on the job how to do—pitch from a stretch. If you pitch from a windup with a man on in the pros, the other team will run wild stealing bases off of you.

The first year a young man leaves home for his career is an important year in his life, but because of the way I was raised, I didn't go out and party or go to bars. I didn't do anything besides play baseball. I had been taught to respect people and treat everybody the way you would like to be treated. I didn't bother anybody. My thing was playing baseball. I knew I needed to have focus and concentration to get ahead. I figured that the lead dog always runs alone. It's the same as when you are hunting. If you have more than one dog, there is always a lead dog and the others follow him. I went my own way.

Every young prospect that has played great in high school and is a No. 1 draft pick believes he is going to be a star in the majors. Some teams don't nurture a young talent and rush players to the big leagues. If you are a young pitcher, of course, that's what you want to happen. You want to go straight to the top and not spend a lot of time in the minors. But most players need that seasoning.

Leaving Lincoln High and Ruston, where I had lived basically a segregated existence—my school being all African Americans—I was also going off to a more integrated world of baseball. Ruston was segregated enough that we couldn't get Ruston High to play sports against us during my time there. The white school wouldn't play us. I always thought part of the reason was that we had better teams, and they didn't want to lose to us.

Race wasn't an issue with me. Discrimination wasn't shown to me directly in Ruston. I never did see prejudice. We stayed in the country and we didn't deal with white people that much. I'm pretty sure there was racism around us in rural Louisiana and through the South since there is still racism out there now, but it wasn't a problem for me. I'm happy when the sun comes up in the morning and I'm alive. I don't owe the world anything except to love.

Racism did not really show itself to me. It was not an issue I heard discussed at my house. It was not an issue in my neighborhood. It was not an issue at my school as a student even if we were all African American, and the other school was all white. Our nearest neighbor was miles away from our house at that time. Nothing big ever happened.

When the season ended in Covington, I had one year of professional baseball under my belt and I went home to Louisiana. I did that for the first few years I played in the minors and then I moved to Houston.

During the offseasons between my minor league seasons, I returned to Ruston and I spent a lot of time fishing and hunting and going for long walks. We hunted for deer and raccoon, and I walked with my uncle. We walked in the woods while hunting. He put his rifle under his arm and could walk for days while raccoon hunting, just following the dogs and listening to them. Out behind the house there was a creek running, and I fished for catfish there. It was about a mile back in the woods. We didn't have fancy fishing rods. We would just break sticks off trees, tie strings on the sticks, and put a hook on. We dug up earthworms for bait and then just threw the line in the water and sat down and waited. If it was bending or jerking, you knew you had something. We reeled the fish in, skinned them, cleaned them, gutted them, and put them in the frying pan. That was dinner.

I learned a lot that first year of baseball, but I also had been shown that I had a long way to go before I made the Astros roster.

5

The Highs and Lows of Triple A

The Houston Astros wanted to be cautious with J.R. Richard's development. They did not want to make a mistake and ruin his potential. They wanted him to be ready for the big leagues when the call was made. After an okay rookie season in the minor leagues, he returned to Louisiana for the offseason and to prepare for season No. 2 in the minors. J.R. spent the summer of 1969 in rookie ball, but in 1970 he started the season at the regular Single A level, one step up.

Richard was assigned to Cocoa in the Florida State League and he spent the season in the Florida heat—not that the weather was much different than what he was used to from growing up in Louisiana. He held a regular spot in the pitching rotation, but Richard experienced a very odd year statistically. His overall record was just 4–11, but his ERA was an excellent 2.39. Once again his strikeout potential was breathtaking. Richard accumulated 138 Ks in 109 innings. His heater was also bad news for opposing batters, who mustered just 67 hits off of him.

The Astros liked what they saw. As he turned 21 in 1971, Richard was ticketed for Triple A ball with Oklahoma City in the American Association. Richard's maturity and all-around pitching development was obvious to see in Oklahoma. He finished 12–7 with a 2.45 ERA and struck out more than 200 batters.

Richard made great strides from his days worrying about rattlesnakes in Covington to taking the mound in the Astrodome, though the journey did include the first of several stops in Oklahoma City and periodic excursions back to Louisiana.

J.R. Richard

When the 1969 season ended in Covington, the team disbanded, and the Astros sent all of us home. They didn't tell me to work on anything or how to spend my time. As spring training approached, I jogged two or three miles a day for my legs, but that was the extent of my working out at the time.

Coming back to Ruston after playing a season of professional baseball was a good experience. People were happy for me, and they were interested in what happened. They really took to me and gave me a nice reception. My youngest brother, Dexter, wanted to follow in my footsteps.

Dexter did become a pretty good ballplayer. He played a lot of sandlot ball. I told him what to do and what not to do. He listened to me and did come to spring training with Houston to see if he could get signed. But he was released and went back home. That was a couple of years into my career. But when I got home, the first summer there was a great reaction. Everybody knew I played ball. Everywhere I went people asked me how it went and wanted to know how I did.

People would say, "You'll make it. You'll move up next year." Coaches in town especially wished me well.

I was not the only good athlete from Ruston. Ralph Garr, who had a very good career as a hitter, was from Ruston and he was already in the majors, mostly playing with the Atlanta Braves. Ralph and I had a competition, a hometown rivalry thing going. Once when I struck him out while he was with Atlanta, he was irate. He was a little older and a good hitter who could run. He always said that he was going to get a hit off of me.

After spending the summer at home, I became a member of the Cocoa, Florida, team. I pitched well, but I did not have a good record (4–11). I didn't give up many runs, but we didn't score very many either. We were not a good team. It's hard to have an earned run average as low as I did and lose that many games. Cocoa was a bit bigger than Covington, and it had a beach going for them. I lived not too far from the water, and I was out more and mingled with a lot more people than I had in Covington. That included being around white people. The whole thing was great. I enjoyed everybody I was around. We seemed to enjoy each other's company. I make friends pretty easily. I got along with everybody. My philosophy is just that you treat me well, and I treat you how I would like to be treated.

The beach was there, and it was very pleasant, but I didn't go all of the time. Being in Florida was pretty much about baseball. I learned how to pitch a lot better, but with my poor overall knowledge, I still needed to pick up more. I wasn't taught a lot about how to pitch a change-up. I basically threw a fastball and a slider. My goal was to overpower people, make them swing at the fastball. But these were better hitters who adjusted, so I had to adjust. It was only going to get tougher as I moved up. I couldn't get by on just a fastball and a slider, so I had to work on a change-up. I knew it would greatly help me if I had an off-speed pitch. That would help me get away with a lot of hard stuff.

One thing I remember about Florida was a near-confrontation with a couple of white players. During batting practice there was an extra batting cage behind second base. A couple of white guys were in there, and they were throwing balls pretty close. We didn't have a fight, but there were some charged words.

There was another incident on a road trip on a bus. A white player took a seat and then got up, and a black player came in and sat down. He didn't want to get up when the white guy got back on the bus. There was a little scrap right there. I, though, kept my nose clean in the minors. I was just trying to get acclimated to the system and I had been taught to play it close. I didn't get involved in anything too exciting.

I played in Virginia and Florida and I didn't really see many real race issues. I never had a problem. One time that race was an issue was when we were finishing spring training one year and driving through New Orleans. We were going to play the first baseball game ever at the Superdome. There was a dinner on the field as part of the special event, and some people who were fans had paid to be there—and may have felt entitled as a result—and they ate at tables with the ballplayers. We were sitting around the table, and one guy just took his catfish and threw it over at my plate. I was really offended. I gave him a few choice words and I had to be taken out of there. It was disrespectful and I couldn't see what motivated him. I didn't appreciate it. It was almost as if he was saying, "Go fetch." It didn't go over real big with me.

I pitched no-hitters all of the time in high school. I threw so many of them I didn't think anything of it. I got used to that, so when I threw a no-hitter against Daytona Beach for Cocoa I didn't think much of anything about that either. It was normal for me. I have never worried about statistics anyway. I never worried about most numbers even later with Houston. I figured if I gave my best everything would fall into place. Even with those 11 defeats, the Astros liked what they saw from me since they promoted me to another classification and a tougher league.

Oklahoma City was the biggest city I had ever lived in up until that point in my life. It has several hundred thousand people and is spread way out. I hadn't had any experience with city life. Oklahoma City really wasn't very far away from Louisiana, and I drove there in my own car for the start of the 1972 season.

Still, in some ways Oklahoma City was also a cow town. For lack of anything better to do, I threw a party where I lived. It was a disco party, just something to do. I think it was a birthday party for my brother coming to town or something like that. I remember getting drunk. I made up some drink that I called "purple passion." We had trash cans full of ice, and we poured in a mixture of Welch's grape juice and everything else around that was 100 proof—vodka, gin, Scotch, whiskey, tequila, wine, some 190 proof grain alcohol. Altogether it was about eight quarts.

I drank and drank, and it tasted good. I didn't really know what I was doing. The next thing I remember is that I was walking through the shallow end of the swimming pool fully dressed. That was some party. I'm not sure Oklahoma City has recovered from it yet. They are still working on it. The next morning I found my brother sitting in a closet with a bucket in front of him in his lap. I think my headache is just starting to go away. I don't know the last time I have had a drink now—it's been years—but I drank sometimes when I was a young player. Afterward, I used to like to run to sweat the alcohol out of my system.

I enjoyed myself in Oklahoma City, but I kept the same attitude, that I was there for baseball and I can't remember one time that I went to a nightclub. I was still a homebody. But I did drink. I drank beer and some alcohol. Not much. Just once in a while. Sometimes I had beers with teammates or once in a while at home. The party was very much an exception. I always was somewhat of a loner. My thinking was that, if you do something here at home, the world doesn't know. The more you do, the more everybody knows.

It's a lot different today with the Internet and YouTube and camera phones. You can't even fart these days. You read about it on the front page of the paper the next day. It's not even just the local paper. You're in *Sports Illustrated*. Everywhere. It's amazing.

My outlook was that I was a professional, and I was getting paid to be a professional. Being a professional is more than acting that way on the field. It's off the field as well as on the field. It's when you are at home and when you are away from home. It's being a professional in public and in private. If you are a professional, you have an image and you should act accordingly.

I grew up with that attitude. I was reared like that, and that's why I didn't trouble anybody. I would hardly ever be seen going into a nightclub when I was a young man. I have to admit a couple of years later when I was being billed as, "J.R. Richard and the Houston Astros," Okay, I started spreading my wings a little bit and started going out a little bit more.

It wasn't that I was ever shy, but I believed big league ballplayers should act a certain way. I had a friend, pitcher Don Wilson, and we talked to a lot of ballplayers and told them they shouldn't do certain things. A special friend of mine that I really admired was John Edwards, the catcher. I respected him and I always remembered things he said to me. He said, "You're a professional ballplayer. Don't do this and don't do that. You don't want to do this. You don't want the publicity." Some mature guys encouraged me in that direction, the right way to behave. They kind of took me under their wings. They showed me what being a big leaguer was all about. They nurtured me along, and I took things they said to heart.

John Edwards had a pretty nice career, and I considered him a good friend. He gave me a lot of knowledge on how to pitch, when to throw certain pitchers, how to pitch in certain situations, and what pitches not to throw in certain situations. He was a real asset to my baseball career. Some of the veterans had an influence on me off the field. He was older and he knew from experience. Those guys told me that it was more important to do what's right off the field than it is on the field because if you get a reputation it's like a bull's-eye on your back. Everybody would be gunning for you with bad publicity, you might be sued in a paternity suit, or whatever the case. A lot of people come after ballplayers and have their hands out for that dollar.

If you are a big league ballplayer, you've got all these crazy girls around who are doing any and everything. Now they want to get you in a position to take your picture and put it on Facebook. Or they want money to keep quiet. It's like that especially if a player is married. I wasn't married in the minors, but I was later with the Astros. There were women out there who came on to you, but they didn't just want to go to bed with a player. They wanted to become part of your life. There was a long line of those times where you heard a woman wanted to get money from a player. They might pretend to be pregnant. They might try to break up a marriage.

There was a little bit of that in the minors, but it intensified in the majors. I was a pretty innocent guy at 19, 20, and 21 in the minors. Sometimes the older fans, who watched those teams for years and years and kept track of the young players who came through and made it to the majors, could be really nice to you. In Cocoa I made friends with an older gentleman named Hilton. I used to go to his house and eat big, old steaks. He was a big baseball fan, and I just had a lot of fun with this guy. He was crazy as all get out. He was a nut. I called him on the phone. We stayed in touch after I left Cocoa up until the time he died.

Oklahoma City was a good place. One thing about Oklahoma City in the summer is that it can get incredibly hot and humid. The humidity could be 100 percent, and the temperature reached 100 degrees. And the weather changed in the afternoon. You could go inside to eat lunch, and it was all sunny and come out and it had gotten cloudy with thunderstorms. The fans liked me, and I pitched well. I was moving up, but I wasn't impatient. Generally, I am a very patient man. I was the Pitcher of the Year then and said, "Well, I should have a shot at the major leagues."

Scipio Spinks, who later played in the majors, was a good friend in Oklahoma City. He was the one who kind of tutored me. My record was 12–7 with a good ERA and a lot of strikeouts. It was not until I had that good season in Oklahoma City that I truly began thinking seriously about making the majors. Of course everyone thinks about it when they get drafted and are in the minors, but it wasn't until I reached a higher level of play and did well there that I let myself really think about the prospects of making it.

My thinking changed. I thought I had pitched well enough to be brought up to the Astros when they needed someone, but instead they brought up Ken Forsch. My record was just as good as his. I couldn't understand why they wouldn't call me up. I talked to someone there and when the Astros didn't bring me up, I said, "Okay, then trade me."

The Astros were shocked when I said that. They immediately said, "What's wrong? What's the problem? You need more money?" They gave me more money. It was actually hush money to be quiet. I kind of let it alone and I realized I was taking my focus off the game a little bit and what I should be doing. I was letting my mind drift away from the business of pitching. I didn't feel I was getting a fair shake. I thought that the team didn't care about me. I was willing to go somewhere else. I felt ready for the majors.

The general manager said, "We can't trade you. What else do you want? What do you need?" They were waiting for me to blossom. It would look bad if they gave up on a No. 1 draft pick and he made it big for another team. After that talk I said, "Okay." Then in September of that year, the Astros did bring me to the majors for the first time and I did well. I showed myself that I belonged in the big leagues. I was only with the Astros for a few weeks, but that's when I knew I was really going to be a big leaguer.

6

A Perilous Ride

Oklahoma City and J.R. Richard developed a very good relationship. In more than one way, Richard's summer stay in Oklahoma City was a bridge stop for him. He got used to hanging out in a city bigger than any he had ever spent time in before and he succeeded so thoroughly in Triple A ball that it was obvious he was going to the majors sooner rather than later.

That was pretty good for a guy who was still just 21 that season. Richard did get the call from the front office that he was going up in September and he made his major league debut on September 5, 1971, pitching against the San Francisco Giants. Over the course of the last weeks of the regular season, Richard started four games for Houston. Although it was not a large enough sample to indicate that Richard was in the bigs for good, all signs pointed in that direction. He went 2–1, and his earned run average was 3.43.

The eye-opener, though, was Richard's performance in his first game. He definitely looked all grown up against the Giants. This was a big moment individually for Richard but also an important moment for the Astros organization and the man they drafted over other worthy candidates. "After we saw J.R., there was no doubt in our minds," said Tal Smith, Houston's director of player personnel at the time. "The raw ability was just awesome in our minds."

Mel Didier—the scouting director of the then-Montreal Expos, the franchise that eventually moved to Washington, D.C. and became the Nationals—convinced Richard to suit up for a throwing workout for him, but since it was not under game conditions, Didier had to round up a catcher. He found a younger kid to handle the duties. "Every time he'd catch one of J.R.'s pitches, it would knock him back about a foot," Didier said. "It was unbelievable the arm that guy had. He was raw, real raw. But you knew if it all came together for him, this boy was going to be something special."

After two seasons in the minors Richard was granted an opportunity to show what he had picked up down on the farm. The Astros' September 5 doubleheader versus the Giants was played at Candlestick Park. During that series Richard would face one of the legends of the game.

J.R. Richard

I struck out a lot of batters—202—for Oklahoma City that summer. My ERA was good, good enough that I probably should have done better than 12–7. But we weren't a good hitting ballclub. With each city and each environment, I was getting more acclimated to bigger cities and I had become a little more outgoing, too, as I was maturing. By the end of the season, I felt as if I was ready to pitch in the major leagues. So did the Astros.

When I was promoted from Oklahoma City, it wasn't just to sit on the bench. They wanted me to pitch to see what

I could do. I wanted to pitch, too. Harry Walker was the manager, and he gave me a couple of days' notice that I was going to start. He said, "You're going to be in the rotation."

I came right to the majors with the team on the road, so I joined the club in San Francisco. The first question that came up was with whom I was going to room. In those days everyone shared rooms. Don Wilson was a good guy and a good pitcher for the Astros. He won 104 games for the team, made an All-Star team, and pitched two no-hitters in the majors.

When I got to San Francisco, Don said, "Okay, I'll room with the rook." He may have technically, but I didn't see Don Wilson at the hotel all weekend. He was out the whole time. It was like rooming by yourself. I wasn't nervous the night before the game even if it was my big league debut, but I did remind myself of the attitude that had brought me this far, about going out and doing my best and being the best. That was always my mantra. And actually that day I was pretty close to the best the way I pitched. I didn't have any relatives there for my start. It was too far away, and there was no time for them to get there. When we went on to Los Angeles to play the Dodgers, I did have some family there.

I knew who some of the Giants were by reputation, but I didn't know who they were to recognize them, and that included Willie Mays. There were no major league games near us when I was growing up in Ruston and there weren't as many games on TV in 1970 as there are now. I just knew it was my job to get the Giants out, and it didn't matter who they were.

The Giants scored two runs off of me in the first inning, but that was almost all they got. We tied it in the third inning and went ahead in the fourth and then added a little bit of a cushion in the fifth. That was enough for us to hang on and win 5–3. I struck out San Francisco catcher Dick Dietz three times and Mays three times and Bobby Bonds twice. After I struck out Mays for the third time, he said something to me. It was kind of like this: "My number is 24. Do you know who wears this number? Do you know who I am? You've got to respect this number."

Well, I respected Willie Mays alright, but I didn't say anything back to him. I could have just said, "Yes, sir, Mr. Mays," but it seemed smarter just not to say a word. Joe Morgan was playing second for us and he came over to the mound and he said the same thing almost. "Do you know who that is?" Morgan laughed when he told me. You don't get to strike out Willie Mays three times in a game too often. I would say that was a feat in itself. It was pretty good for a rookie and there was all this attention on my first game. The game got a lot of publicity.

Right away there was a lot of talk about who was this guy and where did he come from. That made me feel good. When I first struck out Mays three times, I didn't think anything about it. I had struck out a lot of people over the years. Striking out three in a half-inning ain't no big deal. I struck out the side lots of times. I was just trying to do my best. I didn't brag about striking out Mays three times and the Giants 15 times, but other people did brag for me.

Since my big game took place in San Francisco, there was considerable attention on me when we came off the road and got back to Houston. I could hear on the radio or read in the newspapers where people were saying, "Who is this guy?" No matter who you are, no matter if you were a No. 1 draft pick in baseball, you almost always spend time in the minors so you kind of get lost to the major league fans for a while.

We had an announcer named Loel Passe for a long time between 1962 and 1976, and he built me up. He developed this phrase about my strikeouts, saying, "Greased another." He kept saying that, and it caught on. Everywhere you went, man, people were saying, "He greased another." That became a signature phrase of his.

When I came up to the bigs, I was at my full height of 6'8" and I probably weighed 220-something pounds. I was about 3 percent body fat, and that came naturally. Later I got up to about 240 pounds, but I was still 3 percent body fat. I had a natural strength. After the Astros brought me up, I looked at it as just another opportunity to pitch. I wasn't as excited as many other players get. I didn't even save any souvenirs from my first game. I was given a game ball, but I have no idea where it is now. At the time I didn't really think I had done something special. I struck out 15 guys, and everybody kept saying, "Man, great job." I didn't have a clue. I was not knowledgeable about anything going on. I had always struck out a lot of guys in games, so it didn't make as big an impression on me about what I had done as maybe it should have. Somebody else thought it was a pretty big deal, or they wouldn't have given me the game ball. They figured the rookie would want it.

That September I did something very stupid. I had a motorcycle, and one day near the end of the season, I was out riding, and a friend was out riding in his car, and we decided to race. We took off going very fast, and I missed a turn. I was going faster than the conditions allowed and I was coming up on a sidewalk where you can enter a frontage road. I said, "I'm just going to take that bank and I'm going to get in-between and make a turn." Then I jumped the curb, but there was a dog right there, and I was trying to miss him. Really, I was just going too fast. I hit a pole, and it was BLAM! It was a sign pole, and when I fell over, my head, my shoulder, and everything else scraped along the road. Luckily, I had on a helmet. My shoulder was skinned up. All of the snaps were just hanging off my helmet.

When I got to the hospital, the diagnosis was that I had dislocated my shoulder. That was my right shoulder—my pitching shoulder. I had only been in the majors for a few weeks, and that was it for me. The doctors immediately started making gloom and doom predictions. They said I would never pitch again because I had messed up my shoulder. There were some bruises on my body, and some places where I scraped off skin, but the big injury was the dislocated shoulder.

I called the Astros, and you would have to say that they weren't very happy campers. I was told that I wasn't supposed to be riding a motorcycle. It wasn't prohibited in my contract, but I think they put it in players' contracts now. I know you can't skydive. The doctors kept saying, "Your career is over. You'll never pitch anymore." That is alarming to hear, though I didn't really believe it. It was very gloomy. My thinking was different. The thought in the back of my mind was that I knew what my body was capable of doing. Just because they said what they said, that didn't mean it was going to be true. I know God has the last word. Man has only his own feelings and the opinions of other human beings. I was convinced that I was going to pitch again. I wasn't worried about that.

I had a pretty long recovery period, but it was about six months until spring training. As soon as I was healthy enough to do it, I went into a rehab program and went to work building my shoulder up, though I didn't stay in Houston to do it. I went home to Louisiana and worked with my uncle, Bill Frost. I worked on my entire upper body to give the shoulder more strength.

That was the last time I rode a motorcycle, and I'm never going to ride one again. The crash wasn't the motorcycle's fault; it was my fault. I was not cautious enough, going too fast, not knowing the bike very well. I had even had a couple of cocktails that night. I could have wrecked my career. *I could have wrecked my life.*

I flew off the motorcycle when I hit the sign pole, and the results could have been much worse for me. The injuries from the motorcycle crash pretty much cost me a year in the majors. I had had a good season pitching for Oklahoma City and I had done well with the Astros in September. They were planning for me to be a regular starter in 1972) based on what they saw, and that's what I believed would happen.

But after I got hurt in the crash, it was slow going getting ready for baseball by the time of spring training and I wasn't as sharp as I should have been. I think everybody in spring training was kind of waiting to see how I would be. That was the deal. Well, I felt great. I didn't have any pain and I was a little surprised by that. I was surprised there was no pain. So I just kept right on tripping along.

After that I had to prove myself all over again in Oklahoma City. I had to prove things to myself. I just went back to Oklahoma and kept on pitching. I didn't exactly know what the organization wanted to see, but they were watching me closely to make sure I hadn't done permanent damage on the motorcycle. They wanted to see for themselves how I was coming out of recovery and rehabilitation. Really, they wanted to make sure I hadn't lost it.

I spent almost the entire season back in Oklahoma, finishing 10–8 with a 3.02 ERA. Although I wasn't quite as dominating, I still struck out 169 batters in 128 innings. It was a hard winter for me getting ready to play again after the shoulder dislocation and it was a hard summer being back in Oklahoma City when I thought I should have been in Houston. I should have been ready to go straight to the Astros out of spring training in 1972.

In September, a whole year later, the Astros brought me up from Oklahoma City again. I figured I was going to be called up. I appeared in four games again, just one of them a start, and finished 1–0. But I got shelled and gave up a lot of runs. My earned run average was 13.50, though it was only for six innings of pitching.

Nothing against Oklahoma City—I liked it there—but I didn't want to be working there again in 1973. I really wanted to become a full-time Astro. After going back to the minors and doing well, and having that stretch again in Houston, looking ahead to the 1973 season, I thought, *It's my time.*

7

Losing Don

The motorcycle accident interrupted J.R. Richard's ascent to the Houston Astros. He had been given a chance to show his stuff in September of 1972 and took advantage of it. He had made good and pretty much sealed a spot on the roster for the next season. Richard had seen enough of Triple A and he had seen enough of Oklahoma City—not because he thought it was a bad place but because he had been there and done that and felt his career had passed it by.

As it so happened Richard's next Triple A assignment was not in Oklahoma City. He was given a change of scenery in 1973, a different Triple A minor league destination. The Denver Bears had become an Astros affiliate, and Jimy Williams managed the Bears that summer. Williams was moving his way up the food chain and would eventually manage the Toronto Blue Jays, the Boston Red Sox, and the Astros.

For Richard, the stopover in Denver was a get-well, get-sharp visit. The Astros wanted him fit and ready and sent him to Triple A to work out any kinks or residual effects from the accident. The 1973 Astros were improving under then-manager Leo Durocher, who eventually would be voted into the Hall of Fame for his bench acumen over the years. They finished 82–80 that season.

Richard moved up to the big club by mid-season and finished 6–2 with a 4.00 ERA. Durocher dabbled with the idea of making Richard a full-time bullpen guy, but that did not appeal to Richard. He pitched in 16 games that season, and 10 of them were starts. Still, Durocher believed that J.R. had the goods. "He's got a big league arm, great stuff," the manager said. "All he has to do is learn to finesse a little bit. He doesn't have to throw the ball as hard as he does on every pitch."

Some major league players who had never heard of J.R. were impressed by his velocity upon their first glimpse of him. One of those was Pittsburgh Pirates pitcher Dave Guisti after Richard topped his club 10–2. "Hey, where'd that guy come from?" Guisti said. "He throws too hard for this league." Guisti had once played for the Astros but missed Richard's drafting by six months. Guisti thought the only other pitcher in the league who might throw as fast and hard as Richard was Tom Seaver.

Around this time, when Richard was making his first lap around the National League, some wags began calling him "High Rise" because of his 6'8" height. Richard already had his momentous debut game with its 15 strikeouts against the San Francisco Giants behind him but had not had many big league outings like it since. On that August day versus the Pirates, Richard allowed just two hits in a complete-game victory over Dock Ellis. J.R. was throwing a shutout until the ninth when Al Oliver clubbed a two-run double. Oliver said chatter had gotten around about Richard's abilities, and the Pirates had scouting reports on J.R. It was as much a warning as a scouting commentary. "Now I've seen him, and everything I heard about him is true," Oliver said.

That's the respect Richard was after, and he considered his Pirates effort to be very encouraging. "This is what I've been waiting for during the past three years," Richard said after the game. "Ever since [my debut against the Giants] I've been waiting to show what I can do. I'm confident I can pitch up here and be a winner."

Coincidentally, J.R.'s first win in 1973 came on June 24, besting the Giants 8–3 in the second game of a doubleheader. The flamethrower looked like his old self, going six innings, allowing just four hits and one run and striking out six. On August 1 against the Los Angeles Dodgers, Richard hurled a five-hit, complete-game shutout with nine strikeouts. He was finding a groove.

That season one opponent that the Astros saw a fair amount of was future Hall of Fame right-hander Ferguson Jenkins. A winner of 284 games, Jenkins was with the Chicago Cubs that season. He and Richard eventually became good friends—and still are today—after meeting through fellow major league pitcher Jim Bibby.

Jenkins, a veteran by then, said Richard's reputation preceded him around the National League. "It was maybe the mid-1970s," Jenkins recalled. "We heard about this tall, lanky kid throwing bullets out there in the Dome. The feeling at the time, though, was that he was a little bit wild, and he didn't know where those bullets were going. But then he got better and became an awesome ballplayer. He threw fastballs so fast the batters didn't see them. The ball was a blur. Then he developed a slider. He had a great slider. He was on the threshold of being a great star."

J.R. Richard

In 1973 I was 23 and started the season with Denver. One day we went out to the field, and it was covered in two feet of snow. It was an off day, not a postponement, but that was impressive. Part of me thought they might shovel the field off and have us do a workout. The snow melted pretty fast, but it was slushy on the field. If a guy hit a fly ball, it might drop in for a base hit because the outfielder couldn't get any traction. It didn't roll. The ball just fell and stuck.

Playing in the Rocky Mountains is like playing in New England in the spring. They should put a dome over Fenway Park.

Denver was a great town. We used to see snow on a regular basis. We were making minor league salaries, and one time a few of us had a rental car and we were trying to save money. We tried to fool the rental company on how many miles we drove and we took the odometer out. But the transmission fluid leaked out. It was cold and rainy that day. We were trying to fix it, trying to pour transmission fluid into this little bitty hole. We did some crazy stuff trying to save money. Minor leaguers are always conscious of money.

I made a couple of friends in Denver, and they taught me the ropes about the city, where to go, and what to do. One guy had a place he liked, and it was tiny. It was not a fancy nightclub, but you could go there and sit and have a beer and talk. It was his favorite watering hole, and nothing exciting ever happened there. He did do a lot of name dropping, though, and he wanted to show you off to the other customers. I didn't care too much for the mountains. I never even got to go fishing while I was in Denver.

I had a stretch at first with Denver when I was not sharp yet, but then it came together well, and the Astros promoted me. It was kind of frustrating for me to be up with the Astros and then down with Oklahoma City, then up with the Astros and down with Denver. I don't recall them telling me to work on anything specific. I didn't have any more injuries, so it wasn't that. My walk ratio wasn't that high by that point, so I wasn't wild. They always came up with an excuse when they sent you down, but they didn't always really tell you anything special. They might just say, "We think you need a little more work, a little more seasoning." What was wrong wasn't specified.

When the Astros brought me up from Denver, I hoped it would be for good. Then there was some talk of making me a reliever, and I was used in relief a little, but I didn't want to be a relief pitcher. I always wanted to start. I didn't have any idea what was going on when they asked me to pitch in relief. I didn't think there was any question that I was a major leaguer by that point. I worked 72 innings for the Astros with 75 strikeouts. I gave up 38 walks, half as many walks as strikeouts, and 54 hits, less than a hit an inning.

Although everybody knows me as J.R. Richard now, it wasn't until the early 1970s with the Astros when Lee May came over from the Cincinnati Reds that I was called by my initials. Until then people mostly used my full name of James Rodney Richard. Lee decided that name was too long, and he started calling me J.R. It stuck.

Definitely, I was a little bit down about it when I started the 1974 season in the minors again, this time in Columbus, Georgia, in Double A. I was out of sorts there for a while, going 5–8 with an ERA of 5.38. But the moment the Astros moved me back to Denver, I was on fire. I went 4–0 and did not give up an earned run in 33 innings. There's nothing like looking at statistics and seeing that your ERA is 0.00. It can't get better than that. They had no choice but to bring me back after that stretch.

It really is something to be on a roll like that. You know you're not going to lose. You've got it completely pulled together. The confidence built and built and built. I was throwing mostly fastballs—not many change-ups and sliders. My catcher was Cliff Johnson. We became teammates on the Astros throughout the 1970s, too. He was a big, strong guy and he was one of those catchers who would throw dirt on the shoes of the hitters.

Cliff played 15 years in the majors, but he was kind of a nut. He would just do things that were totally crazy. One time we went out to a nightclub in Montreal, Canada, when we were there to play the Expos. He knew a guy there who supplied girls on demand for certain guys he knew. I was rooming with Cliff at the time. A girl was back in our room, and he did some stuff. The girl said, "If I had a gun right now, I'd kill you." That's when I stopped rooming with Cliff Johnson.

He disrespected people. He cursed all of the time, and I stopped hanging around with him because it wasn't in my character. In those days everybody had a roommate, but I started rooming by myself and paying the difference. I didn't care what it cost. I didn't want to get shot and killed because of something crazy he did.

The pitching couldn't have been better. You don't see 33 scoreless innings too often. There was nothing to prove in the minors after that. Still, they wanted to use me in relief when I got back. I couldn't see that. I felt something had to change. I was a starter. I couldn't understand the reasoning. I got back with the Astros and appeared in 15 games, but only nine of them were starts, and I finished 2–3.

The back and forth between the minors and the majors was starting to wear me out, but my feeling was that I wasn't going to let them wear me out. I realized God is the source of all my strength. The Astros didn't wake me up in the morning. That was up to God. The Astros didn't make my heart beat. They didn't put me to sleep at night. They didn't regulate my eyesight or my blood pressure. I couldn't depend on them for that. No man could. I knew I couldn't depend on man for anything. Man doesn't do any of those things. Man doesn't stop the sun from coming up in the morning.

I did wonder what the Astros' plan was for me. I just didn't understand what was going on in the organization. After the Denver stretch, I had to believe there was no reason for me ever to play for a minor league team again. I had a feeling the Astros were holding me back. But I couldn't figure out why that would be. I didn't know why.

The reason I thought that it might be good for me to be traded was the same as how you feel about watching TV. When a show comes on that you don't want to watch, you change the channel. I thought it might be time for a change of scenery for me. I wasn't as young as I had been when they drafted me. I had aged from 19 to 24. I wasn't a teenager anymore. I was a man. I had matured quite a bit since the Astros first drafted me. I thought maybe my talent could be used better somewhere else.

I wasn't sure who was making the decisions, and there was a good reason for that, I guess. The team finished with an 81–81 record. The general manager was Spec Richardson, and the manager was Preston Gomez, but right after that, things fell apart. The team finished last in 1975, and that season started with Richardson as general manager and ended up with Tal Smith. Gomez was out as manager, too. He was replaced by Bill Virdon. There was a bit of turmoil in management that year.

While I was getting impatient, I was disappointed in the Astros. I didn't get angry. I never really get angry. I have never been angry at the Houston Astros. That's not the right word. I've been disappointed with the Astros at times but never angry. I don't know who actually made the decision to leave me in the minors as long as I stayed there and who made the decision to try me in the bullpen. I don't think it was owner Roy Hofheinz. I think he took care of the money side. With a baseball team, one person doesn't control everything. That's why he has other executives.

The worst thing that happened after the end of the 1974 season—and before spring training started the next year in 1975—was the death of my friend Don Wilson. There was always some mystery attached to what happened. It was said that he was intoxicated, but he drove his car into the garage at his home, and there was a fence only a couple of inches away on either side. Somehow he negotiated that completely straight without crashing his car, but then they say that he parked his car, let the garage door down, and went to sleep with the motor running. The police did not rule it a suicide. I heard lots of things that didn't seem to make sense.

The police said that his wife called to him from the house, but she didn't come downstairs to see why he didn't come in. There was a swimming pool right there next to the garage. If he was so intoxicated, how did he miss putting the car in the water and drive so perfectly straight that he missed the walls of the garage? I wasn't there, but if the man was able to avoid the swimming pool, drive on a straight line into the garage safely, and put down the garage door, you would think he would turn off the car.

When I was younger, I came home drunk a few times. The first thing you do when you park is to cut the car off and then stumble out of the car and check to see if your door is locked. That's the first thing you do. You don't sit there. Are you telling me that he got out of his car, pulled down the garage door, and got back into his car and went to sleep? It's not logical. No, it's more logical to crash into the garage wall if you are that intoxicated.

Don was only 29. We were good friends, and his death hit me like a ton of bricks. The Astros called to let me know he died instead of me hearing it on the news first. That was a big loss, and it still bothers me to this day how they described what happened. I keep repeating it because of the lack of logic. It's not a great thing to get that intoxicated and drive at all, but to do what they said he did? Come on now.

It is also hard to think that Don might have killed himself. I never saw any indication that he would. Don had a lot of talent. He made an All-Star team and he actually pitched two no-hitters in the majors. Not many guys ever pitch one. When he was a rookie in 1967, Don pitched a no-hitter against the Atlanta Braves and won the game 2–0. That was the first no-hitter ever thrown in a dome and on artificial turf. Don struck out 15 men in that game and he ended the game by striking out Hank Aaron.

My friend Ralph Garr, who grew up in Ruston and played for the Braves, once told me that Hank Aaron was afraid to hit against me. It was near the end of his career, and he said I threw too hard. He was probably nervous I might hit him in the batter's box. That's the psychological warfare for a pitcher and why you don't let the hitter dig in.

But back to Don, in May of 1969, he pitched his second no-hitter, beating the Cincinnati Reds 4–0. You know what was incredible about that? Just the day before, the Reds' Jim Maloney pitched a no-hitter against the Astros and won 10–0. How would you like to have had tickets for that series? The last game that Don ever pitched at the end of the 1974 season was a two-hit shutout over the Braves. He was pitching great right up to the end of his career and up to what turned out to be the end of his life.

We were good friends, and our wives were good friends. I missed him especially as a friend, more even than I missed him as a teammate and pitcher. I had been somewhat of a loner, so I didn't have many good friends and I did lose a good friend when Don Wilson died. It is a sad thing to say, but after Don passed away during the offseason, the Astros were going to need me more than ever in 1975. When I went to spring training in 1975, I was sure that I was going to stick with the team.

8

Married with Children

As spring training opened for the Houston Astros in February of 1975, J.R. Richard was the object of much speculation and the focus of several newspaper stories. The Houston Post, Houston Chronicle, and The Sporting News charted his progress. It looked as if he was going to be an important cog in the Astros' pitching rotation.

The tragedy of Don Wilson's death was still a raw wound, and many were still grieving his absence. But the team had to play its schedule, and that meant that a new starting pitcher was needed to fill Wilson's role. Richard was the obvious candidate to step in. He knew it, and the team knew it. "He's an important person to this ballclub," Astros general manager John Mullen told a reporter. "He has to step in there and live up to his potential. A job is there to be won, and I think J.R. knows it, too."

As a bit of fine-tuning and as a bridge to a permanent spot in the majors, Richard played winter ball in the Dominican Republic and excelled in the role. He went 8–4 with a 1.50 ERA and, of course, led his league in strikeouts.

From the moment he was drafted by the Astros with that No. 1 pick in 1969, Richard had been a star-in-waiting. Periodically, Houston sportswriters checked on his progress and wrote stories about him. He had experienced those cameos for partial seasons and hinted at his great potential with that overwhelming showing against the San Francisco Giants. Now it seemed it was going to be his turn to shine.

Probably the biggest obstacle Richard had to overcome was the motorcycle accident that separated his right shoulder. The injury that doctors felt might shut down his career did not reach that catastrophic a level, but it was slow to heal. Mullen, who had gone to the Dominican to evaluate Richard's progress, believed that the long recovery had taken root at last. He liked what he saw and felt Richard was back on track. Mullen thought that the injury may have forced Richard to adapt with some off-speed pitches and the combination of his fastball and other stuff would make him better than ever.

Richard did find a home in the Astros' rotation in 1975. He finished 12–10, though his ERA of 4.39 did not make him happy. He struck out 176 men who couldn't handle his fastball, but he was wilder than expected—or than he wanted to be—with a National League-leading 138 walks and 20 wild pitches. One thing that could be guaranteed with his speed and those misses off the center of the plate was that nobody was going to be digging in at the batter's box.

Richard joined an Astros team that had long been an expansion team doormat but was on the rise. He made lifelong friends with some of his teammates, including third baseman Enos Cabell. The 1975 season was Cabell's first with the Astros, and he and J.R. were teammates for six years. They met in the minors, but Cabell was always in another organization. They didn't become teammates until they both alighted on the Astros' roster. "I first met J.R. in 1969 in rookie league," Cabell said. "He was playing in Covington, Virginia, and I was in Bluefield. It was the same league, and I was introduced to him by a mutual friend. The same friend introduced me to my wife. J.R. and I were opponents then, but I never had to hit against J.R. I was lucky. I got to watch him throw. These were small towns with teams a long time ago, and they didn't all have the fanciest facilities. I watched J.R. throw batting practice, and the batting cage was made of chicken wire. His fastball was going through the chicken wire. After I saw that, I said to myself, 'I don't know if I want to face this guy. If he hits me with a pitch, I'm in trouble.' He never pitched against us in a game, thank God." Cabell said he refused to hit against Richard even when it didn't count. "They'd have to pay me to hit against him," Cabell said. "I wouldn't hit against him in batting practice."

J.R. Richard

I went to the Dominican Republic in winter and played for Estrellas. It was my first time out of the country, and playing winter ball was good for me. I remember Gary Matthews was playing there when I was. So was Ed Armbrister, who was from the Bahamas, and later played for the Cincinnati Reds.

Over there baseball is a totally different thing. I went out there to strike guys out, and the batters came out swinging. They swung at the high pitch. The atmosphere was rowdy and fun. You might be in the middle of a game, and a chicken would run across the field. Guys would chase after that chicken that had escaped. Two minutes later you would see smoke, and it was coming from where they were cooking that chicken. It smelled pretty good, too.

On one road trip we ran into a guy, and I guess he didn't have all of his faculties. A bird fell out of its nest, a little baby, and a guy on the team told this other guy that he would give him $5 if he ate the bird. So he stuffed it in his mouth. He didn't cook it. There was blood running out of his mouth as he chewed on this little bitty bird.

My Spanish was not particularly good. Mostly I knew bad words, but I also could speak enough to get by. I learned it there. I had to. I started attending church there with some of the local people. I get along with most people. I even started speaking in church.

It was a very different culture. The best nightclub for the players to visit was also a whorehouse. It was a club and a whorehouse. I didn't go there for the girls.

There was a slaughterhouse built right next to the ocean, and as they were processing meat, they cut out any unborn calves and just threw them into the water. Then you would see these big old sharks come rolling over. The processing plant had umpteen jillion flies. The workers would butcher the animals and stand in blood a foot deep on the floor. They waded along in blood. The meat went right from there to the butcher shop.

I didn't trust all of the food available in restaurants. I used to go into the kitchen of the hotel I was staying at and eat cheese dough instead of going out. I ate with the kitchen workers and had a great time. I enjoyed the people in the Dominican a lot.

Whenever I got paid, I took my check to the bank and cashed it and loaded up my pockets with change. The kids would always be asking you for money, and I threw the change to them in the road. There would just be a few of them around and suddenly there were tons of kids coming out of nowhere. The people in the bank knew what I was doing and they started calling me "El Grande," the big man. I was the biggest guy around.

It was a great winter, a great place to be sent to pitch. The country was not wealthy, and you could live like a king on a little bit of money. I met some of the rich folks, too, and they owned ranches. I used to ride horses there. There were also a lot of Americans around. There was a pretty good-sized population of Americans studying at medical school, including quite a few New Yorkers. They might not have been able to get into med school in the states, but they wanted to be doctors and went to the Dominican to train.

The atmosphere in the park was loud, and everyone wanted to have a good time. The baseball was fine. I enjoyed the game. There was a lot of betting going on each team during the games. In the capital the teams had older women—not teenaged girls—as cheerleaders. But they were really dance teams and they danced on top of the dugout roofs. It was as if it was Las Vegas and it was a strip club. It was awesome in its own way.

I remember the Alou brothers—Felipe, Matty, and Jesus— from the Dominican Republic, and, of course, Juan Marichal. When I was there, some of the players chewed on something they called "buckeye seeds." In the U.S. players chew sunflower seeds. There was some kind of superstition about buckeye seeds. They said it affected you like marijuana and you could see the spirits.

My time in the Dominican was about 40 years ago, and Dominican baseball has changed so much. Back then there were only a small number of big leaguers from the Dominican Republic. Now there are like a zillion guys who have made it. Teams have whole organizations there. They have baseball camps for teenagers with dormitories. Sixteen-year-olds with potential go there.

Baseball is much more sophisticated in the Dominican than it was when I played there. Many ballplayers have made a lot of money in the majors and gone home and given back to their communities. I saw young guys playing on fields that had a lot of rocks on them. They had holes on them. They were nothing fields. I saw a guy trying to field a ground ball and get hit in the face when it took a bad bounce. He got a bloody nose, but he picked up the ball, threw the runner out, and said, "Let's go." Baseball was a way of life, and it was a harder way of life then.

Everyone in the Dominican knows now that if there is a son in the family and he is discovered by a major league team, he can play, get rich, and lift the entire extended family from poverty forever. Some players come to the U.S. and bring their whole families over. Being able to play baseball changes their whole world.

My manager that winter in the Dominican was Hub Kittle. Hub spent almost his whole life in baseball. He pitched in the minors for 21 years and he even took the mound once when he was 63. That made him the only player to pitch in five decades. He was a coach for several years for the Astros and the St. Louis Cardinals. I heard once that someone called him the "Santa Claus of pitching coaches" because he had a bag of tricks like a bag of toys. Hub worked with me a lot in the Dominican. Overall, I just really enjoyed the local people there. It was a good winter.

When I went to spring training this time, I knew I was staying with the team. Before 1975 I was never sure that was going to be the case. I only hoped it would be the case. The opportunity was there. There were some openings in the starting rotation.

I gave myself a pep talk. I didn't say it out loud or make any boasts. I thought, *Okay, this is my chance.* I just kept playing hard, trying to show everybody I was doing my best. I ran as much as I could. I did little things to perfect my game. If I thought I had a weakness in my fielding, I worked on my fielding. I worked on every weakness I thought I might have and tried to turn it into a strength. I did improve my fielding, and it helped a lot. There are times when you are going to have a line drive shooting off the bat at you, and the only thing you can do is jump out of the way, but if your reflexes are good enough, you can try to catch it, too.

That is the most dangerous thing for a pitcher. I have seen highlights on ESPN where guys just throw their glove up and catch the ball an inch from their face. One time I saw a pitcher catch a liner behind his back. One pitcher I played with had a line drive hit him right in the nuts. It was a line drive up the middle that was smoked, and he just folded up. He had to leave the game. I wonder if he could have children after that.

I changed my delivery to improve my balance after I threw the ball so I would be in better position to field. I used to have a delivery where on my follow-through I'd be way off the mound like Bob Gibson was, leaning over to one side, falling to one side. I changed my step from inside to using more of the outside of my back heel so I would have better balance in my legs at the end of my delivery. When I landed I had better balance and I could react to a ball hit at me. I was originally so off-balance that if a ball was hit hard back at me I didn't have time to react to it. I had to duck and take my chances.

If I had been batting against Gibson, I might have tried to bunt at him where he was falling over to just tire him out, just keep bunting and tiring him out fielding. I worked very hard to make myself a better fielder. I knew it would eventually pay off and it did.

Spring training ended, and I knew I wasn't going to Denver. I wasn't going to Columbus, Georgia. I wasn't going to Oklahoma City. I was going to Houston. I thought *I am in the major leagues now. Let me show them what I can do.* Everything started clicking. Every year I pitched, I got better and better. My control got better, and I increased my strikeout percentage.

I finally bought a house in Houston in the same neighborhood as some of my teammates. Enos Cabell was a very good friend of mine when we played together and he still is today. We met in the minors and became good friends when we played together with the Astros. We teased each other, talked trash. Like me he was trying to develop consistency. Enos had a lot of confidence and he would brag about what a great hitter he was even when his batting average wasn't that great. He had a pretty good career, but when Enos got like that, I would tease him by saying things like, "You play every day, and I've got more home runs than you do."

At this time I got married to my first wife, Carolyn, who was my high school sweetheart. I was 20 when we got married. I was coming out of rookie ball. I've been married three times now. I became a father at a young age, too. Carolyn and I had a daughter, Paula, right away. I have five children. Paula was the first, and my other daughter is Crystal. There are three boys: Eric, Patrick, and James. I also have a stepdaughter Zanna, who is not my biological child. The kids are pretty much in their 30s and early 40s.

One of my chief forms of relaxation has always been fishing, but I also equate baseball with relaxation. The muscles cannot work when they are tight. They've got to be loosey-goosey to work to their maximum efficiency. That was always one of my pet peeves when I was pitching. I wanted to work for maximum efficiency and I believed to obtain that you could not be tense and not be doing a whole lot of thinking that distracted you. I was at my best when I was reacting.

That was something I had to learn with experience. It came a little bit later in life—not when I first started pitching. When you are young, you basically want to throw the ball as hard as you can. But you don't throw as hard if your muscles are tight. I experimented with it. It's like when you go out and overdo something. It may be because everything is out of proportion. The movements weren't natural. Things become irregular and don't make sense. All of the pieces don't connect with each other.

If you're in a tense situation on the field, the natural thing is to think about what's going on out there and what you've got to do. But the correct tendency is to go ahead and be yourself. Don't worry about this and that and the other if you don't get this guy at the plate out. If a guy is on base, you can't worry about what will happen and if someone hits it there he'll score. Just concentrate, just be concerned about the hitter at the plate, and forget what's going on out in the field.

As a pitcher you have to realize if the guy at the plate doesn't get on, nobody is going anywhere. If you get him out, the inning's over. So what's more important? Is it the guy at the plate or the guy at second base? The time for thinking is when he first comes up to the plate. You look at a certain hitter and if you know he's a fastball hitter and he likes it low and inside, you don't throw the guy a fastball where he likes it. You throw it anywhere but low and inside. Most left-handed hitters, when they hold their hands high, can't hit the low ball. If you throw the ball high to low-ball hitters, they can't touch it. A high-ball hitter can drop down and hit the ball, but if they have to drop their shoulder to adjust, usually it's too late. The ball is by them already.

It was interesting to be a young father and a young pitcher who was still trying to make it. I was never a partier, so it wasn't as if I missed going out to nightclubs all of the time. I was pretty much a stay-at-home guy anyway. There were challenges. It was great in a sense with the kids, but I was out there laying it on the line and focused on my baseball career, trying to make money, and take care of them. I didn't have time to issue them the love that I should have. I didn't have the time to give the kids the attention they deserved because that meant stopping what I was doing to get ahead in baseball. I should have spent more time with them and doing things with them.

My career was baseball, and every time I tried to watch the kids do something or go to one of their events, baseball came up. That was especially true during the season when you're really busy and traveling out of town and not seeing them at home. Then in the offseason they went to school, and there wasn't as much time to interact as I would have liked. I know I didn't spend enough time with my daughters because of my career. I spent a little more time with my sons because I took them fishing and doing sports type things like that.

I was young and I didn't know how to handle both things at once to give the kids enough attention and still get ahead in baseball. My father didn't show much love to us, and I didn't show enough love to my kids. It was something passed on from generation to generation. You realize these things later. I learned this over the years and I am trying to break that generational habit.

You have to ask yourself if it was really worth it, sacrificing your family for the game. In some ways it wasn't. I want to apologize to my kids and say that I'm sorry. I didn't understand things then, but I understand things now. You always look at the money aspect and then you say it was worth it. But if you look at the love aspect, it wasn't worth it because that part of your life you miss. You're supposed to be close to your family. Then you think about it later in life and you grieve about it. You don't harp on it because what's the use of harping? That has happened. You can't go back and change it. The only thing that you do is you try to make up for it, do what you can do starting now. Back then is gone. It will never be there again, but in the here and now, you try to issue them love. If the kids have a bad attitude over it, it's just tougher. The closeness isn't there, and you have to try. It's tough. I feel that it is a parent's duty to correct and protect their children. God gave them that right, and it's a way of showing love.

As a professional athlete, you have to pour a tremendous amount of effort into it to try to be the best. It requires you to invest a tremendous amount of time. There are difficult choices. It can create a lot of animosity, but when you are 19, 20, 21, you have to do certain things right then if you are going to advance as a baseball player. When I was that age, I didn't know how to be a parent, but as I have grown older, I understand what parenting is all about.

There's also the fact that when you grow older, and your father and mother die, you think, *I could have done this. I could have done that. I could have spent more time with them, showed them more love. I could have thrown them a surprise birthday party.* I think about those things, but at the same time life goes on. Life carries on.

I was married to my first wife for about 10 years. We got together in high school, and I thought we would always be together. But sometimes it's your destination to end up in a different place. Some say life is all a trip, but I think it's about the destination. I was destined to play baseball, but it was a sacrifice.

It's kind of a Catch-22. If I had not played baseball and we didn't have money, we wouldn't have lived in the house we lived in, we wouldn't have had the money to buy the school clothes they wanted. So you're always pitting one against the other. If you don't throw the water out of the boat, you're going to sink. If you throw the water out of the boat, you aren't going to catch as many fish because you're too busy bailing the water out of the boat. It's always one thing against the other. You try to maintain.

If I had never become a professional baseball player, I probably still would have become a professional athlete, probably in basketball, though I would have gone to college on a scholarship out of high school instead of going into the minors.

It's funny because some boys dream of becoming a policeman or a fireman when they are young. I wanted to be a truck driver when I grew up. That was my idea of a good job. I thought about driving trucks because I liked how they looked. I obviously didn't know what it took to be a truck driver or to get into the profession.

I can say all of this from the perspective of being in my 60s now and going through all of the things in life that I have gone through. But when I was 21, it didn't seem that there was much to think about. You have a role to play in life and you play that role. Your role might be the foot, so you don't try to be the hand. I think I chose the right sport to play. Definitely at the time, it was the right decision. I haven't changed my mind. Baseball was the right sport, though maybe I could have been in a different organization.

You couldn't control what team chose you in the draft in 1969 and you can't control it now. Over time I developed the thought that the New York Yankees were the best organization to be with and play for. They almost always have a good team and they seemed to have appreciation for older players. They don't just take older players and throw them away. They use the older players to help the young kids, which is good. The young kids coming to the majors need some guidance to help break them into the game and show them how to be a big leaguer.

It was very satisfying to me when I became a big leaguer for good in 1975. I made it for a full season. Though I knew I could play better, I thought I was well-positioned to keep improving and helping the Astros become a better team. The Astros were a bad team in 1975 with a record of 64–97. We had a long way to go. That left us in sixth place in the National League West Division, so the only way to go was up.

9

The Lion in the Valley

From the time J.R. Richard made his much-talked-about debut in his taming of the San Francisco Giants, there was little doubt that he was on his way to a permanent starring role with the Houston Astros. It was just a matter of time and seasoning.

Richard gained a little bit more big league experience each season, and the Astros gave him a little bit more time in the majors each year. He was weary of airplanes that took him around the country for different assignments. He wanted to sink his spikes into the ground in Houston and stay there.

The 1975 season was Richard's breakthrough when he won 12 games and remained with the Astros the entire year. Richard entered the team's starting rotation with the full intention of remaining there for a long time. This was the true beginning of the J.R. Richard era in Houston, when fans, who had been hearing about him for years and had only caught glimpses of him in a series of what amounted to cameo appearances, now had the chance to watch him pitch every fourth day.

The 1975 season was prelude to the 20-win season of 1976, the year when Richard and his whiplash arm firing bullets at nervous batters began making his reputation for real. Richard was no longer just one of the guys who trotted out to take a turn on the mound. He was easing into the role of The Guy, the pitcher the Astros relied on the most. Throughout baseball history, even during the Deadball Era when pitchers threw more complete games, pitched with less rest, and won up to 40 games in a season, it was always a signal of accomplishment to win 20 games.

The 20-victory plateau has been an even more prized achievement in recent years since the sport has emphasized the relief pitcher, devalued the complete game, and shifted to five-man rotations. Twenty wins is one of the most noteworthy milestones that a starting pitcher can point to as evidence that he had a fine season in the majors.

Although he was unaware of it at the time because the special club did not yet exist at the time, J.R. Richard's 20 wins marked a different sort of rare accomplishment. The Black Aces is a fraternity that owes its origins to former big league pitcher Jim "Mudcat" Grant. Not only did Grant write a book of the same name, but he has perpetuated the club's continuing existence to draw attention to the exploits of African American pitchers.

Given how long Major League Baseball has been around—since 1876—and given how many outstanding African American pitchers there have been, Grant's study of the history shows that only a small number of them have ever won 20 games. Part of the reason is that black players were unofficially (with no written rule) but basically banned from participation in the majors from 1889 to 1947.

Grant played in the majors for 14 seasons between 1958 and 1971, winning 145 games, primarily for the Cleveland Indians and Minnesota, though also notching wins for a handful of other teams. The 6'1" right-hander finished 21–7 for the Twins in 1965, leading the American League in victories and gaining one of his two All-Star mentions. In his book introduction, Grant noted of The Black Aces, "It is important to them that history remembers the fact that they succeed in an arena where no other blacks had been allowed to even enter...they were successful pitchers period. They were incredible athletes, fierce competitors, and highly accomplished professionals."

Grant was nearing the end of his career and made an appearance as player-coach in the minors with the Iowa Oaks in 1971 when he stumbled across Richard throwing for Oklahoma City. The first thing Grant did was telephone to Oakland Athletics owner Charlie Finley and gush that he had to try to obtain Richard some way. Grant was awed by Richard's stuff, saying, "James Rodney Richard, one of the few men I know big enough to have three first names."

J.R. Richard

By the time I became a full-time starter for the Astros in 1975, it seemed as if a long time had passed since my debut with the team beating the Giants in 1971. In the years in between, I had gained maturity. Besides a fastball and slider, I now brought assurance to the table. Once I got to the majors full-time, I was committed to using all my power to stay there. I definitely wanted to be on the top of my game, to bring all of my talent and knowledge to making progress and knowing how to pitch.

I learned through experience, and it took time. It was a question of going around the league and seeing all of the hitters and learning their tendencies. You had to learn what to throw to guys in different situations and understand the differences in their strengths and weaknesses. One guy was a low-ball hitter, and the next guy was a high-ball hitter. Most left-handed hitters love a pitch that's low and away. My fastball was my No. 1 weapon most of the time, but sometimes it could be the slider. In some starts it would be vice versa. It was more like 1 and 1A. It took a long time to truly master a change-up and develop that niche.

I had a change-up, but I needed to disguise it better. My delivery needed improvement as far as showing and telling. I found out how to do it. That's the key. Nothing changes in your delivery with a fastball and a change-up. It has to come out the same. It's just how the pitch comes off your fingers. You may change the number of fingers you use and you can't throw it as hard. The delivery has to look the same, but you don't have the same force behind the pitch. The change-up is a deception pitch. Batters didn't have much time to react to my fastball. They had to make up their minds to swing as the ball left my hand. For the hitter, hopefully his bat hits the ball.

I was always committed to trying to throw a complete game. I threw seven complete games in 1975 and 14 in 1976. When I went out to the mound I told the relievers, "Y'all, take the day off today." A lot of sportswriters kept commenting on my potential. One article had some comments from Johnny Edwards, who caught me a lot and who was one of my favorites to work with. He said, "He has such a live arm. I can just motion to him and say, 'Take it easy.'"

Everyone thought I was so big, but when I was at 220 pounds or so, I felt skinny. I did a lot of running. If I didn't feel strong or think I was in great shape, I was running, running, running to build stamina. Managers and coaches always say that a pitcher's strength comes from his legs. That's why if you go out early to the park for a major league game and watch batting practice, you'll also see pitchers running around the outfield perimeter near the fences.

You use your legs when you pitch, and if you don't have strong legs, eventually you get out of rhythm, and your shoulder will give out. You have to stay in shape with your legs, but I also think the stomach provides a lot of energy for your whole body. Energy comes from there. The legs and abs are part of your balance when you follow through on a pitch. If you just throw with your arm, you lose speed.

At the end of spring training in 1975, I knew I was going to be in the rotation. I said to myself, "I'm staying in Houston. No more Oklahoma City. This is it." I had a very positive attitude in spring training. I thought, *How many kids playing baseball would give a part of their lives to have my arm or be in the position I'm in?* I reached a point where I started cherishing what I had, where I was, and the opportunity I was being given. You start thinking about being grateful and being honored at the position you are in.

I had had a taste of the big leagues starting in 1971. I felt in my heart it was going to get better. I always asked the manager and coaches, "Where am I weak at?" I was facing guys like Pete Rose for the first time. But by 1975 my attitude had firmed up. I went out there to the mound thinking, *I'm the baddest lion in the valley and you have to beat me.* I was friendly enough to other players but not when it came to games. I am a competitor, and my attitude was not to give anyone a chance. Winning—that's what I wanted to do when I went out there. We could play a game right now, and I would still feel that I was going to win. Back then, most of the time I did.

Baseball has never wanted players on different teams to fraternize, but I talked to some of the hitters. One player from another team that I became good friends with was Dusty Baker. Dusty was playing outfield for the Atlanta Braves at the time and then he became an All-Star with the Los Angeles Dodgers. After that he had a great managing career. He actually gave me some advice, even though he would have to hit against me. He occasionally said I should do this or that, and it would make me more effective. Most of the guys I talked to, teammates or not, talked a lot about using my off-speed pitch. I started using it later in my career as my control got better. Most people came up to bat expecting a fastball, which they couldn't catch up to, but later I mixed the change-up in more and that fooled them.

That was my job—to keep the hitters off-balance. You really throw them off-balance if you have a good change-up. I already knew I could throw a fastball for a strike at any time. I used to set up the hitters by throwing inside and then throwing a slider even more inside. If I got two strikes, I would come back and bust him in again. By then the hitter was expecting a pitch outside. They were trying to guess what I was going to throw, and I was trying to keep them off-balance. The two best pitches in baseball are the fastball and the change-up if the hitter can't tell them apart or judge them leaving your hand. Plus, the change-up may be as much as 20 mph slower, depending on who is throwing it. The hitter's timing is way off. They can't do a thing with it, or if they hit the ball, it's just a weak grounder or something like that.

Fans are fooled by change-ups in a way, too. A lot of times they see a slow pitch coming up to the plate and think, *Why can't that guy just kill it?* But most times the pitch paralyzes the hitter. If you are known for your fastball and they see a good fastball, that's what they are set for. The pitch isn't even close to the plate, and they flail at it. The timing really had an effect. When I first saw hitters completely fooled and swinging at my slow stuff, it made a big impact on me. It really dawned on me how important it could be. I remember a guy with the Giants who had such a devastating change-up because of the mph difference from his fastball. But he also had a pitch that was even slower. Guys were swinging at air.

One guy who is great at that in the majors these days is Bronson Arroyo, who was with the Cincinnati Reds for a long time and now is with the Arizona Diamondbacks. His fastball isn't that fast, just the high 80s, but his change-up might be 69 mph. That's like knuckleball speed. There's no way a hitter can time him when you throw a 16 mph difference in the pitches. Sometimes the difference is 20 mph. That's way out there.

That 1975 season was a learning season about more than pitching. That's when I really learned how to be a professional off the field as well as on the field. I prided myself on improving. I wanted to be a complete player, fielding, bunting, hitting, as well as pitching, the whole nine yards. Anything that had to do with pitching I wanted to soak up. I didn't want any holes. I didn't want to have any weaknesses.

In 1975 Larry Dierker was the Opening Day starter, and I got my first win on April 20 against the Reds. It was far from my best game ever. I went eight and two-third innings and gave up five runs and walked eight. We somehow won 7–6. My next win was a lot neater. I went the distance and gave up only five hits. We beat the San Diego Padres 8–2, and I even had a hit and two runs batted in. Pitchers love to talk big about their hitting.

It takes time to establish yourself in the majors, but I started to do that in 1975. I won 12 games and I pitched 203 innings for the Astros that year after pitching 64⅔ innings for them the year before. I'm establishing myself. You have to keep working on your own game, but you can never stop learning or keeping up with the rest of the year. Each year there were new guys in the league that came along. I had to learn about new individual hitters and make adjustments. I did a lot of talking to older guys during the 1975 season. Young guys come up to the majors, and they don't know from a hill of beans what to do. They don't know anything.

When it comes to young hitters, they are like young pitchers. They have to learn from experience. You want to be consistent. You have to be if you are going to be a star and you want the big money. Some guys never learn, and their whole career is like that. They alternate hitting home runs and striking out. They don't work to get better. It takes time, but you don't have much time. You know what I mean? Tomorrow is not promised. I should know that better than anybody. Prepare for tomorrow.

For the 1976 season, I got the Opening Day start for the Astros, which was an honor. It said a lot to me when I became the Opening Day starter. But I didn't have a good day, and we lost 11–5. Four days later I got my first win of the season. I went five and two-third innings and didn't give up any runs, but I walked seven. We beat the Giants 5–0. I actually started very well and was 5–1 on May 7 after we beat the St. Louis Cardinals 3–1. I only gave up six hits.

Complete games were important to me. Every time I went out to the mound, my philosophy was that I was going to be there for all nine innings. I prepared myself for that. The game was scheduled for nine innings, but it might go 15 innings, and I was ready for that if need be. Some games I got stronger, the longer I was in there. After that fast start, though, I went into a slump and I woke up after a game on May 31 and I was only 5–5.

I didn't always have a lot of luck in every game I pitched that season. On June 14 I lost 2–1 to the Pittsburgh Pirates. Jerry Reuss went the distance against me. I gave up two runs on five hits with two walks in seven and two-third innings, but I took the loss. Less than two weeks later, I lost 1–0 to the Dodgers and Rick Rhoden. He pitched a three-hit shutout. I gave up two hits and one run in eight innings. After that game my record was 7–8 with a 2.96 ERA.

Boy, my July 6 game against the New York Mets was a crazy one. I won the game 1–0 in 10 innings, but I walked 10 guys and gave up eight hits. There were base runners all over the place, but somehow I didn't let them score. I wonder how many pitches I threw that day. They didn't track them back then like they do now.

But after that things took off. I started getting it all together. Everything jelled. It became a great year, and I won 20 games. In July, August, and the first half of September, it was wild. Almost every game I was in was a close one, a one-run game or a two-run game. I beat the Montreal Expos twice—4–2 and 3–1. I beat Atlanta 2–1 and the Dodgers 1–0. I beat the Chicago Cubs 5–3 and the Philadelphia Phillies 3–2. There was almost always pressure. In that 3–1 Expos game the only run was unearned. In the Atlanta game on July 31 as part of a doubleheader, the Braves' only run was unearned also. In the Phillies game, only one of their two runs was earned. When I beat the Dodgers 1–0 in August, I struck out 10.

Closing it out in September, the push for 20 wins was fascinating. I beat the Giants 14–5. (I always seemed to have good wins over San Francisco.) Then I had another 1–0 victory against the Dodgers for my 19th win. That was a three-hit shutout that barely took two hours. Burt Hooton for the Dodgers only gave up four hits and one run, and that one was unearned. That was September 28 and ordinarily that would have been my last start of the regular season, but manager Bill Virdon adjusted the rotation to let me take a shot at 20 wins, and I am forever grateful that he did. That season my confidence grew by leaps. Sometimes batters even knew what was coming with my fastball and they still couldn't do anything with it.

People started to talk about me differently. On my best days, I heard them say, "He's unhittable." I even started hearing that some batters didn't want to play on the days I was scheduled to pitch. I started a new disease called "J.R.-itis. Not trying to be boastful, but they were taking a day off, a sick day.

When I started to win almost every game for a while in July and August, it was like dominoes falling. I was coming into my own. A lot of that was the confidence factor. When you pitch well and win and you keep winning, it makes you feel that you are unbeatable. I started to feel like I was the best in the world. That's a very important attitude to have for an athlete in competition. It's not about having a swelled head, but it's about thinking that if you play your best nobody can stop you.

The mental part of sports is a huge thing. If you don't believe you are the best, you won't be. That's why I talk about the lion being the baddest thing in the valley. He has got to let other animals and people know to stay away from his territory. He feels and believes he is the biggest and the baddest out there. You have to be sure of your talent. You don't say anything. Let the other people talk about you. That was my thing: to prepare myself, to get my rest, and do what I needed to do. Don't go out on a road trip and stay out drinking and fornicating and staying up late when you are scheduled to pitch. I stayed within my own little area, mostly staying in the house or the hotel so I could prepare myself for tomorrow. Anyone who stayed out all night drinking and then went to bed couldn't feel good for the game. Some of the young guys felt they were invincible, but they were putting wear and tear on their bodies. Even if they overcame it right then, later on in life and in their careers it was going to catch up to them.

That season I was the Astros' Most Valuable Player. I felt as if I had arrived after all of my years of work. There were a lot of articles written about me around the league, and players were saying, "Man, you know how incredible you are?" You could hear fans say, "Oh, God, look, there he is." One time I took my son out to the movies, and the line was like two days long. The people recognized me and let us in. That's pretty nice to have a privilege like that, but later I worried that maybe that's not a good lesson for my kids. I didn't want him going around saying things like, "I'm J.R. Richard's son, so let me in." I finished 20–15. It was, "Okay, I'm on top now."

There was no talk of The Black Aces when I won 20 games, but later, when Jim "Mudcat" Grant got things going, it was an honor to be one of the African Americans who had done it. I was in very good company. The guy I wish I had seen pitch was Satchel Paige. I would have loved to see him in his prime. This man, he was unbelievable, the best. I read where he would practice, do warm-ups, when he put something like a gum wrapper on home plate and throw the ball over it. He had pinpoint control.

Many times I wish that I could have seen some of the stars of the Negro Leagues play. Satchel Paige, Josh Gibson, those other pitchers in The Black Aces. They say that Josh Gibson could hit the ball a country mile. There were so many of those Negro Leagues stars that played the game so well but never got the exposure by playing in the majors because of discrimination.

I don't know what's going on in baseball now. Blacks were banned for so long, and when Jackie Robinson broke into the majors, it was the biggest thing going on in the country. Now there are fewer and fewer African American players. A lot of good athletes choose to go into basketball and football instead of baseball. I actually saw an article or heard on TV that only 8 percent of major league players are black. I wonder if there is some discrimination factor at work in drafting. Being part of The Black Aces is something I am proud of, but I'm surprised there aren't more African American 20-game winners.

10

20 Victories

On the last day of the 1976 major league season, James Rodney Richard, known to fans of the Houston Astros as J.R., reached a personal milestone. It was October 2, a day when the weather didn't matter, even if the calendar had turned to autumn because the game was played inside the Houston Astrodome, the showcase stadium that some called the Eighth Wonder of the World, or at least the modern world. There was no doubt that it was definitely a wonder of the sports world and it also heralded long-term change, leading to more and more domed stadiums eventually being built.

The day's entertainment was a baseball game between the Astros and the San Francisco Giants. It was a meaningless game in the big picture of the National League standings. Both teams had losing records, and after the players showered and changed and the clubhouse door swung shut, the door would also close on the season. Neither squad would advance to the NL Championship Series or the World Series.

But it was a far from meaningless day for Richard. His performance on the mound symbolized the entirety of his pitching career to that point in his 26 years on Earth. He had been waiting a long time for this moment to prove something to himself, to fans, and to baseball observers. It wasn't much of a game from a competitive or dramatic standpoint either. Probably the only one feeling any pressure at all, other than daydreaming about how they were going to cram all of their clothes into their suitcase space, was Richard.

In 1969 the Astros drafted the Louisiana-born Richard on the faith that he would one day be a star hurler for them. Richard was the team's first pick in the amateur draft, the second player chosen overall. Scouts who recommend investing a high first-round pick on a player have done their homework. They have studied the young player's results, tendencies, friends, family, coaches, and concluded that he has the right stuff, that he will make good for the big club.

Richard, who had been a superstar athlete in three sports in high school, shined so brightly that he even earned the sometimes-risky label of "Can't miss." He was a raw-boned, all-around athlete of considerable size, standing 6'8" and eventually bulking up to a muscular 240 pounds. Radar guns were invented for law enforcement agencies handling speeders on the highway and introduced in the 1940s. It was the 1960s before they were in widespread use in baseball. Still, the sophistication of pitch timing on radar guns was not yet viewed as 100 percent reliable when Richard was breaking into the majors. In the 1970s technology was improving to the point where they were being trusted more.

With his big gun of a right arm, Richard was one of the pitchers whose speed was the object of fascination for fans. It was generally conceded that he could throw 100 mph, and that's how Houston fans talked about him. Richard made his major league debut in 1971, but seeking more consistency and control, the Astros used him mostly in cameo roles for a few years. Richard joined the rotation in 1975 and became an ace in 1976.

The American Bicentennial year represented Richard's true breakthrough, and he reached the tail-end of the season standing one win shy of 20 victories. Richard had pitched a 1–0 shutout against the Los Angeles Dodgers on September 28 and ordinarily that would have been the last start of his season.

Manager Bill Virdon, however, decided to give Richard a shot at 20 wins, the magic number for all pitchers. The game may have been played in a climate-controlled environment, but the Giants were well aware of the strong breezes blowing as Richard's fastball roared past them.

J.R. Richard

Winning 20 games was a goal I had set for myself when I made the majors. It was the last day of the season, and we were all going home for the off-season after that game. Our record was 79–82. The San Francisco Giants' record was 74–87. It had not been a great year for either team. The size of the crowd reflected that, too. There were hardly any fans there because it was the end of the season and we were out of it. We weren't a very good ballclub. I bet, though, now there are 50,000 fans who say they were there. You might say that the fans had pretty much packed up for the season as well. The attendance that day was 7,612. The Astrodome was pretty empty that day.

Winning 20 games for any starting pitcher is a milestone, and it is getting harder and harder to do now since pitchers throw every fifth day instead of every fourth day and relief pitchers come in earlier and earlier. They talk about pitching six innings and giving up three runs or less as a "quality" start. When we took the ball, our intention was to throw nine innings and not give up any runs.

If you become a major league pitcher who wins 20 games, then you have reached a milestone, and you kind of can write your own epitaph in baseball. It stays with you. It's a milestone that doesn't ever go away, especially if you are a young pitcher, and you do it for the first time, it's "Okay, this guy is here. He won 20 games."

It is not that easy to win 20 games when you are playing for a team that isn't very good. I won 20 games with a mediocre ballclub. We won 80, and that means I won 25 percent of all our wins that season. My earned run average was 2.75. Pitching that well for a team that didn't score a lot and didn't win a lot, I'd have to think I might have won 25 games or more with a pennant winner.

But that day all I was thinking about was how I was getting a chance to reach a very big goal on the last day of the season. I think manager Bill Virdon booted someone out of the rotation for me. It was a four-man rotation, and we usually pitched every fourth day, but I didn't care if I had to pitch on two days rest. I could do it.

I was not a particularly great hitting pitcher, and that year my average was .140. The designated hitter hadn't yet come in—that was a couple of years away—but the National League never adopted it anyway, so I always had to hit throughout my career. One funny thing about that season was that the opposing hitters' average against me was almost the same as mine. It was .146.

My fans do remember this game because of the 20th win, and so do I, but one thing they don't always recall is that I also hit a home run. It came in the sixth inning off of a Giants pitcher named Tommy Toms. Overall, it was one of the best hitting days I ever had in the majors. I got three hits that day and had three runs batted in.

You know pitchers always like to talk about their hitting, but that wasn't the most important element of my game that day. The Giants scored a run first in the top of the first inning. I got a little mad at myself and said, *If you're going to win this game, it's going to be 1–0 because you ain't getting no more runs.* I shifted my focus on them and I developed a concrete attitude. I felt as if I was willing to give my life for that game. I shut them down the rest of the way.

We won the game 10–1. The Giants didn't get much of anything else off of me. We scored four runs in the bottom of the second inning to take the lead, scored four more in the sixth inning, and added a couple of more runs here and there. I pitched a four-hitter, and four different Giants got one hit each off of me. The most I was tagged for was one double.

You know who had a big game for us? Our second baseman was a guy named Rob Andrews, who was only with the Astros for two seasons and didn't have a very long major league career. But he was our leadoff hitter that day and he got three hits. Bob Watson, who is still a good friend of mine, knocked in two runs that day and so did Cliff Johnson. Jose Cruz, another longtime friend, had two hits. The guys came through for me.

I pitched a complete game and struck out 13. The Giants used a lot of pitchers to make it through. Compared to these days when games last much longer, I cruised. The game was over in two hours, eight minutes. You hardly ever see a big league game go that fast now, never in the playoffs.

Going into the game, I felt so psyched up because I was going after my 20th win. I was adamant that I was going to get it. I was young and strong and felt I could pitch any time the manager wanted me, never mind waiting for four days rest. It felt as if everything was on the line and I hung it all out there.

One thing about the way I pitched. Once the catcher threw the ball back to me I didn't waste time on the mound. I got the sign from the catcher and I was ready to go. Most of the batters didn't step out of the box and adjust batting gloves or helmets as often as they do now. There wasn't a whole lot of time wasting unless the hitter was trying to dig a hole in the box. If I saw a hitter doing that I thought, *So, you're digging in, huh? I don't know why you're digging in against me.* If a hitter was digging in I'd go, *What are you thinking?* If a batter is digging in it's almost as if he was taunting you. I figured he was wasting his time because he wasn't going to be standing in that spot very long.

It didn't bother me at all to go inside and make the ball run in on purpose to make him aware of what he was doing. It was going to be high inside, sent as a reminder that I was the one in charge. My livelihood was in their hands, but their life was in my hands. I could end their career or lives if I pitched high and inside with my fastball, or I could break a rib if I hit them in the side where they had no protection. They weren't going to be dug in. They were going to be ducking out of the way.

I didn't want to hit them, but I wasn't above brushing them back and sending a message. Sometimes they were going to fall down to get out of the way and throw the stick up in the air. One thing about being a dominating pitcher is that you are in control.

Once I got in a rhythm, I wanted to pitch. Catch the ball, read the sign, and throw it again. I didn't want batters fooling around up there. Sometimes somebody didn't get the message and they were still digging in. You didn't do that. I had to establish myself just like Hall of Famer Bob Gibson did. A batter who digs in against you, that's a sign of disrespect. You couldn't let them get a toehold and set up just where they wanted to be. Sometimes you didn't even believe it if a hitter got right back up and dug in all over again. I'd think, *You're digging your own grave.* He was asking for trouble if he tried to hog the plate.

When that game ended, I had my 20th win and I was proud. It was the first time I won 20 games in the big leagues and I thought for sure it was just a start and that I would win 20 lots of times. You can never predict how things will go in life, and that turned out to be the only time. I did think I would win 20 games in a season many times after that. I looked at it as being a beginning.

I was young and strong. I threw 14 complete games that year and figured out that was the secret to winning a lot—keep the ball out of the hands of the bullpen. You're the starter. Stay in the game and finish what you started. Am I supposed to win or am I supposed to lose? If I lose I want it to be my fault, not someone else's fault.

As it turned out, I won 20 in a season just once. We can all speak hypothetically about what should have happened and what would have happened, if life had gone this way instead of that way. God loves you, and sometimes he does things that change your life in a way you don't expect. But he changes it because he loves you. My one 20-win season was special, and I will always treasure that game.

11

300 Strikeouts

After all of his patience and practice, J.R. Richard had established himself as one of the best pitchers in baseball in 1976 with his 20-win season. When discussion turned to J.R., it often provoked comments about the ridiculous difficulty of hitting his fastball. It had also become pretty clear to hitters that they shouldn't dig in on Richard, or if they did, they should make sure their health premiums were paid up.

Although J.R. did not win 20 games again in 1977, his all-around season was just as good. His record was 18–12. His earned run average was 2.97. For the second year in a row, Richard struck out 214 men. He also lowered his walks total by 47. Baseball people started looking at him through appreciative eyes. Richard was no longer potential waiting to bust out. At 27 he was in his prime and he was a very important man in the rotation for the 81–81 Astros, who were working hard to build a winning club.

That season Houston had a core group of first-rate hitters, several of whom have remained close friends of J.R's. That group included Bob Watson, who hit 22 home runs and knocked in 110 runs while batting .289; Jose Cruz, who hit 17 home runs, drove in 87, and batted .299; and Enos Cabell, who smacked 16 home runs and batted .282. The Astros also had Cesar Cedeno, who added some pop with 14 homers and a .279 average.

Behind Richard the four-man rotation did not perform very well, but spot starter Joe Niekro, the knuckleball maven, helped considerably, finishing 13–8 with a 3.04 ERA. "The big stars did not want to hit against J.R.," Cabell said. "He's throwing 98 to 100 mph. Even though they didn't have radar guns routinely until the latter part of his career, he was blazing. He had two types of sliders…J.R. was so big and his hands were so big, he pulled his hat down over his face, and you couldn't really see him. That made him even more intimidating. When he pitched we knew we were going to win."

Richard made 36 starts that season and threw 13 complete games. He resisted leaving almost all of the others. "He never came out of games," Cabell said. "It seemed he always pitched nine innings. In addition to being that big, J.R. was very agile. That meant he could do things athletically that other people his size couldn't do."

One of the most beloved Astros was pitcher Larry Dierker, who was winning 20 games for Houston in 1969 when the Astros made Richard their No. 1 draft pick. Dierker kept winning through the 1970s as J.R. broke in and slowly worked his way up to star status. A two-time All-Star, Dierker managed the Astros later after winning 137 games for the team and also served as a longtime broadcaster. He is pretty much Mr. Astro in Houston. "I believe the first time I saw J.R. was his first spring training with the Astros," Dierker said. "He was definitely a first-round draft pick talent and then some. He wasn't as consistent yet, but his athleticism was a pretty impressive package. He was extremely fast, but he was wild."

Dierker was one of those pitchers who enjoyed taking his cuts and he remembers a spring training trip to Orlando when the Astros were scheduled to play the Minnesota Twins. Richard was throwing batting practice. "I had to step in there against J.R.," Dierker said. "I like to hit. But I don't like to hit that much. He was the most intimidating pitcher against right-handed hitters that I saw. His delivery wasn't completely straight over the top. It was three-quarters. He scared guys. The only reason to stay in the batter's box was to collect a paycheck."

Richard made it pretty tough to earn those paychecks.

One pretty solid hitter, Richie Hebner, the 18-year major leaguer who played third base for the Pittsburgh Pirates and other teams, once said of the combination of Richard's fastball and his delivery, "He is so close to the plate when he finishes his windup that I'm thankful he didn't eat onions before the game."

Richard had a little bit of trouble stringing together wins at the beginning of the 1977 season as did the Astros. Based on attendance the Houston fans did not demonstrate much belief in the team. In a May 20 game at the Astrodome, 8,892 fans turned up for an attractive pitching match-up between J.R. and the Philadelphia Phillies' future Hall of Famer Steve Carlton. In a game that took just one hour, 54 minutes to play, Richard pitched a complete-game, surrendering only two runs. Carlton gave up all of the runs in a 5–2 Houston triumph.

That victory seemed to propel J.R. in the right direction. He began clicking off low-run wins, giving up a run or two here or there. Then he got hotter, shutting out the Cincinnati Reds twice within a week. The first game, on July 11, was a 2–0 whitewash. That was a five-hitter. On July 16, J.R. gave up four hits in six innings. That was against a Big Red Machine batting order, too, with Pete Rose, Johnny Bench, Ken Griffey, George Foster, and Joe Morgan. Every one of those guys had been All-Stars in their careers and all were chosen for the National League All-Star team that season.

That season Richard blanked the Montreal Expos 4–0 on three hits and the San Diego Padres 11–0 on three hits as well. In 1978 Richard won 18 games again, finishing 18–11 with a 3.11 ERA. He threw 275 innings that year, but his strikeout total exploded to 303. As of 2014 there have been 64 occasions when a major league pitcher has struck out at least 300 batters in one season. However, 34 of those marks were recorded before 1900, before the modern era of baseball, and during a time period when the rules were different from the present day and fluctuated, too.

The modern strikeout record of 383 was established by Nolan Ryan in 1973. Ryan, who was a Richard teammate with the Astros, struck out 300 batters in a season six times and holds the all-time career mark of 5,714 strikeouts. When J.R. struck out 303 batters in 1978 he joined an exclusive post-1900 fraternity of pitchers that had reached that milestone. Ryan, Sandy Koufax, Mickey Lolich, Rube Waddell, Walter Johnson, Bob Feller, Sam McDowell, Steve Carlton, and Vida Blue were the only others. Blue and Richard were part of a special club within a special fraternity. "J.R. is my homeboy," Vida Blue said. "He and I are the only two Black Aces with 300 strikeouts in a season. I think he did it twice."

J.R. Richard

The 20-win season really put me at a new, higher level, and I started winning a lot of games every year for the rest of the 1970s following that season. My ERA was getting lower, and I was striking out more guys, too.

Those were good days. I kept improving. I kept getting better and I worked to get better. From the playing days of Babe Ruth on, the home run was always the big thing for hitters. For pitchers, the strikeout was kind of like that. It showed you were a power pitcher and you had mastery over the batters. Deep down, yes, I have to admit, it was really fun to strike guys out.

It was enjoyable. It was mine. I had definitely been labeled a power pitcher, and that's what I was. I thought it was something to be proud of and so was striking guys out. Most of the guys who had struck out 300 guys before me played in the American League, and most of them were left-handed. Bob Gibson had never done it. I couldn't believe I did something that Bob Gibson didn't do. This was a small club, and it was a pretty rare thing in baseball history, so it makes it kind of the exception to the rule.

A pretty big deal was made out of things when I hit 290 strikeouts in September of 1978 in a game against the Atlanta Braves. It broke the record for a right-handed National League pitcher. Tom Seaver had struck out 289 batters. They had me pose for a picture holding a baseball with "290" written on it. I struck out 11 batters that game, and my 290th of the season was Rowland Office.

I remember saying that more people took note of me getting 290 strikeouts in 1978 than noticed me winning 20 games in a season in 1976. I was also the first black pitcher in the National League to get to 290 strikeouts. I felt good about the record and I felt pride in doing something African Americans hadn't done yet. I thought it was good to bring attention to my accomplishment for black kids. I hoped it would be noticed by a younger generation of African

Americans. I wanted them to get the message that they could do anything they wanted to do and nothing would hold them back as long as they put their minds to it. The only thing standing in the way of them achieving great things was themselves.

Everyone has to have pride in what they do, and if they lose their pride, they give up and they are on their own. If you haven't got that, you're going to go out there and shrivel up and die. Pride is going to keep you going. It took me eight years after I was drafted, eight years of ups and downs to reach that point where I started winning a lot and gaining some recognition.

That season I was on a roll. The Astros had not been a very good team and did not get a lot of national recognition. Although 290 wasn't a magic number like 300 strikeouts, it brought me a surprising amount of attention. I had wanted to be the No. 1 guy on the team pitching, and after I struck out the 290th batter, *The Sporting News* and TV stations started saying, "J.R. Richard and the Houston Astros." It was like being the star of a movie with my name on the marquee above the name of the picture. I thought, *Now I'm getting recognition.* It had taken a long time, almost a whole decade.

It felt great, but I didn't feel as if I had come from a disadvantaged situation and had to overcome my background or anything like that. We weren't rich, but I had good parents who instilled good lessons in me. The big thing to me was the steady improvement. Year after year I worked hard at getting better and I felt I was still getting better. I felt if I had pitched longer my control would have been devastating against hitters. My command would get better.

An intimidating presence on the mound, I won 107 games during my 10 years with the Astros. (Courtesy National Baseball Hall of Fame Library, Cooperstown, New York)

I stride toward the plate during my major league career, which included 1,493 strikeouts. (Courtesy National Baseball Hall of Fame Library, Cooperstown, New York)

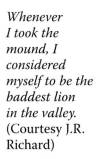

Whenever I took the mound, I considered myself to be the baddest lion in the valley. (Courtesy J.R. Richard)

I take great pride in having recorded 303 strikeouts in 1978. That's a single-season mark that pitchers in today's game rarely reach. (Newscom)

To demonstrate my long fingers and large hands, a photographer suggested I hold all of these baseballs in this 1979 picture. (Courtesy Houston Astros)

Nolan Ryan joined me on the Astros staff in 1980, giving our team two of the most powerful and intimidating pitchers of our generation.

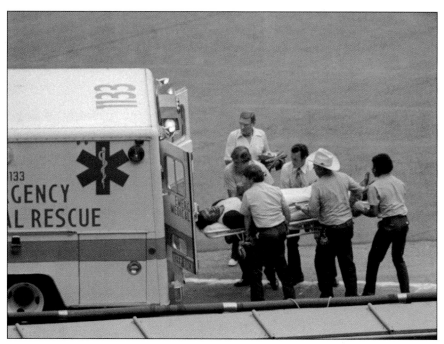

After a light workout at the Astrodome on July 30, 1980, I collapsed on the field and was rushed to the hospital via an ambulance. I was diagnosed with a stroke, which would ultimately end my playing career. (AP Images)

I pose with Astros television commentator Bill Brown during my induction into the Astros Walk of Fame in June of 2012.

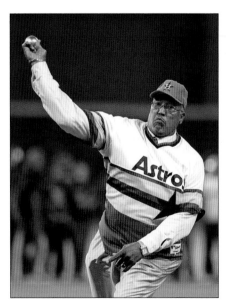

I throw out the ceremonial first pitch during that same June game when the Astros inducted me into their Wall of Fame.

Former Astros stars Shane Reynolds and Jeff Bagwell (No. 5) look on while I wrestle with my old friend, Jose Cruz, during a pregame ceremony in September of 2012, which honored the Astros' all-time roster.

I pose with my former coach, Robert Smith, who remains a mentor to me to this day. (Courtesy Lew Freedman)

Coach Robert Smith and I stand beside Buddy "OK" Davis, a longtime Ruston, Louisiana, sportswriter. Davis recently suffered a stroke, so I've been able to relay my own personal experience as he fights to recover. (Courtesy Lew Freedman)

My life is now better than ever because of the love of my life, Lula, who I met at a Houston-area church. (Courtesy Lula Richard)

After the 20-game season, I won 18 games the next year and 18 games the year after that. To me I was showing people that it wasn't a fluke, that it wasn't an accident. I didn't make the All-Star team in those years yet. Part of the reason was that I had slow starts and came on strong in the second half of the season and won more games after the All-Star Game than before it when the voting was going on and managers were making the selections.

I ended up with 303 strikeouts in 1978. For a while after that, some good pitchers like Curt Schilling, Randy Johnson, Pedro Martinez, and Mike Scott, another Astro, joined the club, but it's not going to happen anymore. Those days of pitchers striking out 300 batters are gone because guys don't pitch enough. Teams protect them. They don't throw the innings they need. Now they use so many relievers who are pitching well, starters still get the hook early. It kind of sucks the way they play today. Given the way baseball has changed with pitchers starting every fifth day instead of every fourth day, surrendering the ball earlier than ever in games to relievers, and having pitch counts that limit their stays in games, the sport may never see a 300-strikeout performance again.

Getting 300 strikeouts at the end of the year got everyone's attention. People started noticing me, even if I didn't play for a winning team. It was great when I got those 300 strikeouts. When I did it in 1978, it put me in a class by myself for the time. I felt great about the accomplishment, but to me the biggest privilege was that I was even in a position to obtain that milestone. I have to give God all of the acclaim for that because if it wasn't for him I wouldn't have made it. He gave me my talent. I thought back on being a poor black boy in the country who got his start throwing rocks at birds and rabbits and who went out in the woods with a club and killed rattlesnakes and wild things.

It's pretty amazing to say that you were a major league pitcher. What a great job to have. I don't know what the odds are of any kid making it to the big leagues. Everybody starts out in little league, and a lot of kids stop playing after that. Then a lot of kids are finished with baseball after high school. They draft hundreds of guys every year and that's only a small percentage of the guys who play high school or college baseball. What are the odds against a player even playing in the minors? Then a lot of good players do well in rookie ball, Class A, Class AA, and even AAA, and they never get an at-bat in the majors or throw a pitch in the big leagues.

It's important for you to appreciate every minute you are on a big league team. They think it is going to go on forever and then they get hurt. Look at all of those pitchers who have Tommy John surgery to fix their arms. There are more of them all of the time getting hurt, it seems. Tommy John surgery saves them, but even if they have the operation, not everyone comes back to full strength.

Athletes are the fittest people around, and they have counted on their bodies to take them to the top, whether it is baseball, basketball, or football, but injuries can ruin a career in a heartbeat. It might seem like something small at first that can be repaired, but there are cases where pitchers twist their back, and when they compensate, they throw out their arms and are never able to pitch as well again.

12

My Years of Domination

The years 1976 through 1979 were superb seasons on the mound for J.R. Richard. He won 20, 18, 18, and 18 games in successive seasons for the Astros. Twice he topped the 300 barrier in strikeouts, leading the National League in that category in 1978 with 303 and in 1979 with 313. J.R. also led the league with a 2.71 ERA in 1979 and in those four years he posted totals of 14, 13, 16, and 19 complete games. During the current modern baseball era, complete games are a lost art. One day versus the Los Angeles Dodgers, Richard tossed 152 pitches, and manager Bill Virdon said he never considered taking him out.

Richard's pitching prowess was a major topic around the NL and around baseball. Opponents and teammates were impressed by what he did on a daily basis and how his blistering fastball enabled him to control games. He was a workhorse thrower, the kind of starting pitcher a manager rolls out every fourth day without worry. Richard didn't get sick, didn't get injured, and didn't miss his pitching turn. He cranked out the starts: 39 in 1976, 36 in 1977, 36 in 1978, 38 in 1979. Richard was the anchor of the Astros' rotation.

J.R.'s only flaw was an occasional lapse into wildness. He did walk more men than was advisable as a general rule, and one day his powerful right arm seemed to go off on a tangent of its own. He threw six wild pitches in one game, a record spanning the 20th century that he didn't wish to own. Yet for all of that, Richard won that game 2–1 (it was the 152-pitch contest) against the Dodgers. "I made all the doctors in Houston some extra money tonight because everybody who saw me pitch probably developed an ulcer," Richard told a sportswriter after the game. Likely he could see the humor in his outing since he won the game. The explanation for the epidemic of wild pitches was Richard losing control of his slider, normally his second best pitch, which he realized he was aiming rather than throwing loosely. The ball repeatedly ended up in the dirt in front of home plate.

It really seemed impossible that the Dodgers did not score more. They had runners on third base practically all night, and once Richard struck out the side with men on second and third. The Astros catcher that day throughout all of the angst who had a front-row seat for an ulcer was Bruce Bochy, the manager who led the San Francisco Giants to three World Series titles between 2010 and 2014.

This was Exhibit A of why catchers are often described as warriors. Afterward, Bochy said he was taking home "about a dozen bruises." Mostly though, J.R. began accruing more acclaim. *The Sporting News* ran a lengthy feature on him by Houston sportswriter Harry Shattuck, calling him "King Richard" in the headline. The story was accompanied by a classic photo of a smiling Richard wearing an Astros cap and with his right hand raised in the air holding eight baseballs simultaneously. It is a mind-boggling shot and illustrates better than anything just how large Richard's hands were.

The picture itself has lived on in Astros lore, and the team passed out postcards featuring it. Richard has autographed many of the photos over the years.

The better Richard got, the more sportswriters fished for stories about him and inevitably they settled on his all-around high school exploits as fodder to demonstrate what a great athlete Richard had always been. It was almost as if they had discovered Paul Bunyan in Louisiana. "Call him the National League's best pitcher, as some do," Shattuck wrote. "Call him baseball's most awesome pitcher, as many do. Call him unpredictable, as all do. But always call him exciting."

Richard always seemed able to handle the West Coast teams, frequently beating both the Giants and Dodgers. At one point he won eight straight games over Los Angeles. They had to hate seeing him coming. "Fastball or slider, 1–2 or 2–1, it doesn't matter," said Dodgers infielder Davey Lopes. "Either way he is the best."

Over time it appeared that Virdon was the one who might develop the ulcers. He had a repeat saying to sportswriters when Richard turned in one of his adventurous games. "It's never easy with J.R.," he said. Richard's pal Enos Cabell admitted that the number of walks made him and other players uneasy, but J.R. usually found a way to pitch out of jams. Richard talked of putting in overtime to improve his fielding, and Cabell said that did happen. "He used to throw games away, beat himself," Cabell said. "His defense is his biggest improvement."

Richard appreciated compliments like that, but he thought beyond physical drills. "I've learned to step off the mound and try to reflect on what is happening to me," Richard said. "[I] try to adjust mentally and physically. And baseball is no different from life. I hope I've matured as a person, too." Richard often used the word "mature" to describe his evolution, tying it to his steady improvement as a pitcher. Still, he always seemed to start even his best seasons slowly and then catch fire during the second half of the season. That cost him All-Star votes. Many times a hot pitcher will zip through the first half of the season, be chosen for the All-Star team, and then falter.

For J.R. things always seemed to work in reverse. After the votes were taken and the game was played, he was so good he toyed with opposing hitters. That pattern was never more in evidence than during the 1979 season. Despite his fine four seasons in a row, Richard had yet to be selected for the All-Star team.

But he certainly produced an All-Star second-half of the season. Over a six-week period, J.R. threw nine complete games in a row, gave up only four earned runs total, went 40 straight innings without surrendering an earned run, and went 8–1, his only loss being 1–0. Cabell was approached by a sportswriter at the time and asked if this was the best he had ever seen Richard, but he wouldn't concede the point. "The year he won 20 games he was nasty," Cabell said. "The year he struck out 300 batters he was nasty. This year he is still nasty."

J.R. Richard

I always wanted to go the distance on the mound. I never wanted to come out. Pitching complete games was important to me. Bill Virdon used to come out of the dugout to talk things over and ask how I was doing. He'd say he was going to take me out, and I would resist. I'd say, "Who do you have in the bullpen who's better than I am?"

You've got a chance to stay in if the manager comes to the mound to talk to you. It's over if he comes out of the dugout signaling to the bullpen. Sometimes I'd talk to Virdon, and he'd agree to let me stay in for another couple of hitters. If I didn't improve or did something wrong after that, he would take me out. He wouldn't be discussing anything if he had to come out a second time. If a manager comes out twice in an inning, you have to go automatically. But I talked my way into some extra time on those first visits.

It would be hard for me to operate in today's pitching climate. They take guys out so fast. I would argue, "Okay, if that's the way you want to do it, but it's not for me. Just let me alone to pitch. I'll tell you when I need to come out, but if I'm doing really well in the game and I've got the score 1–0, don't bother me."

These days a pitcher might be going along with a four-hitter and he's thrown 112 pitches, and they take him out in the ninth inning with one or two outs to go. That's crazy. If the guy is pitching fine, let him pitch. If he gets in trouble, take him out quickly. If he's going okay, let him stay in. Sometimes you let pitchers pitch out of a jam and get out of the trouble. It's better for the team in the long run if he stays in. Sometimes he is going to get beaten up. If a guy walks the first batter of the inning, that never looks good. I know that. If he starts walking guys, that is a sign of fatigue, and you take him out. In one game during the 1978 season, I pitched 11 innings and I struck out 10, though I lost it. It was a complete game. These days I wouldn't have come close. They would have had me out of there by the eighth inning for sure.

Going into the 1979 season, I was definitely at the top of my game. I had put together three excellent seasons and I was loaded with confidence. I was sweating confidence out of my pores. That year I had a weird game against the Dodgers that I won 2–1, even though I threw six wild pitches. I have no idea what was going on that day. It was a crazy game. Even though I won the game, I tried to put it out of my mind as soon as possible. I chalked it up to a bad day. I would throw a wild pitch, get in trouble with the runners, and then strike out three guys. I did it again, throwing a wild pitch, having a lot of guys on base, and then struck out two to get out of the inning. I never had another game like that.

I struck out at least 10 guys in a game 14 times, and that's how I got to 300 strikeouts. Thinking of that brings a smile to my face. I wanted to be the No. 1 pitcher on the staff and I think I was. One thing that was interesting was how the Astros had me in the rotation throwing 100 mph and Joe Niekro throwing a knuckleball like 65 mph or something like that. If we pitched back-to-back in the same series, that had to drive batters crazy.

We were getting a lot better as a team, too, and finished 89–73 in 1979. Then we added Nolan Ryan in 1980. So as a pitching staff, we could start J.R. Richard throwing 100 mph, put Joe Niekro second, throwing 65 mph, and come back with Nolan Ryan throwing 100 mph. Try dealing with that lineup in a three-game series. The combination would just drive hitters wild.

Going back to 1979, we just didn't score enough runs. No doubt about it. If we could have hit more, we would have had a great record, and I bet my pitching record would have been 24–7 instead of 18–13 with my 2.71 ERA. Some days I used to think I had to drive in a run myself to have a chance to win.

I liked to think that I was a pretty good hitting pitcher, and then I get reminded that Babe Ruth started out as a pitcher and won almost 100 games before he switched over to hitting full-time. Now there was a guy who could hit a ton. Now we have Barry Bonds as the all-time home run hitter. His father, Bobby Bonds, played when I did. Barry has such a negative image. I talked to him about it, and he said that he had spoken with a reporter, and the reporter wrote some things that he didn't say that made him look bad. Then he just said, "Okay, the heck with it, I won't talk to any of them." So he is made to look like an a-hole.

But he's one of the greatest players I've ever seen. He should be in the Hall of Fame based on his record alone. But they have rules. There's no doubt in my mind that Pete Rose should be in the Hall of Fame, but if you break the rules, it can eliminate you from everything else, all of the other accolades you might get. Some guys took performance-enhancing drugs to make $50 million a contract. If they didn't take the juice, they would have made $25 million. That was in their minds. The way I look at it, taking the juice was an excuse for not working hard. You could have made improvements by leaps and bounds by hard work. My feeling is that the guy who took the juice used an artificial method when he could have accomplished the same thing with hard work.

I don't care how much juice you take, it doesn't better equip you for hand-eye coordination. You don't hear anything about Hank Aaron taking anything. He never bulked up. Some of these guys got all swollen up. Nobody said anything. There was nothing like that going on that I was aware of when I was playing. I didn't hear of anybody taking steroids. Players used to take uppers before a game to get going if they had had a bad night the night before, out drinking, out with a woman, or not sleeping.

I think Rose should be in the Hall of Fame. I think they've got to let Bonds in, Roger Clemens, Mark McGwire, Sammy Sosa, and Rafael Palmeiro. It's all kind of crazy, though. I was fascinated by New York Yankees pitcher Andy Pettitte. He said, "I tried steroids for a while. They didn't work and I quit." He came back and pitched after that, and you never heard anything else about it. I think he said, "I've got to stand up in front of God" and tell his story. A lot of guys stood up and lied about it and were totally dishonest. I can't do that. Congress held hearings and knew some of them took drugs. They had all of the evidence. They had evidence but no proof.

I've seen players go on a road trip for two weeks, and they party and do whatever and they come home and bring their wives a present, and everything is good and normal at home. How you behave has a lot to do with how you were raised. I have been married three times, but my belief is that you should do all that you can to stay married. A lot of times it is better for the kids. In a sense it is good that a player who fools around on the road stays married. It's good in a sense, but morally it is terrible.

By 1979 I had become much better known outside of Houston. I was recognized everywhere I went, and people wanted my autograph. I don't know what life is like for rock stars, but it got to the point with me that I couldn't go out to a restaurant. I had to eat dinner in my room every night on the road. Everyone wanted to meet me. They wanted me to do this and that. I had to find more private surroundings. People want to be part of you. When you checked into a hotel, you had to change your name. I used fake names to register. I heard of other players using fake names like Fred Flintstone, but I just made up names like Charlie Something. People were following me. It would have been a hoot to use Fred Flintstone, but that would have just given it away. I just made up names. This was before cell phones, and I don't think hotels worked as hard to keep your privacy yet either. Now if you don't take your cell phone with you, if you leave it at home, you're lost.

After I began winning many games and striking out many guys, newspaper articles started getting pretty extravagant. One called me "King Richard." I felt like a king. The king is the commander. He's the chief, commander-in-chief. Reading that felt good. I liked what my teammate Enos Cabell said about me being nasty pitching for a few years in different ways. I liked to hear that kind of thing. Sure, it's recognition. If someone is talking about you being the best, whatever sport it is, it speaks volumes. It's the way people talked about Michael Jordan in basketball, or Kareem Abdul-Jabbar before Jordan, and LeBron James after him. When people talk about you as if you are a dominator, then it feels good.

If you started to believe your own publicity too much, though, you'd think you could just walk out of the dugout to the mound, throw your glove out there, and get everybody out. I never took it to that extreme. I couldn't take the praise for granted, but I enjoyed it when I heard it. I still respected the opposing batters. I respected them all, but feared none.

It was during that time in 1979 when I posed for the picture with all of the baseballs in my hand. I always did have big hands, but somebody said that I must have put glue on the baseballs to hold them all together. There was no glue. The picture was taken by someone with the Astros, though it has been used in a lot of places. I never tried to see how many I could hold at once. I never tried anything like that before. It must have been the photographer's idea. They were just regular baseballs, and I could hold them between my fingers. I was smiling in the picture to show how comfortable I was, how easy it was.

I have long fingers, and that helped me with my pitching, too. It gave me control and it made the ball move a lot. It was an asset. Having big hands helped me out in basketball. I could palm the ball, and it was easier to direct it where I wanted it to go. The size of my hands helped me throw a football, too. It was always a plus. I'm sure that my size came from my grandfather on my mother's side. He stood about 6'10". His name was Feelow Frost. My dad was not very tall. He was of average height. My mother was six feet, which is tall for a woman.

Big hands, long arms, that's what I've got and I always did. In high school football, when the other team tried to tackle me, I could stiff-arm guys and I could stand wide-legged. They couldn't get both of my legs to tackle me, and I stood there and threw the ball all over the yard. I think playing baseball was a God-given ability, but my physical assets helped and so did hard work. From the time I was young, people—coaches, players, women—commented on the size of my hands. The women say, "I just love those hands." And I say, "I bet you do. So does my wife." I love that picture of me holding the baseballs.

When I had the hot stretch after the All-Star break in 1979, everything was getting better and better and better. Everything was jelling. Rhythm was important. There were no lapses in concentration. My focus was good. I was getting everyone out and I was relaxed. If you overdo it, your muscles don't work well together. They work separately. But if you're loose, then it comes together.

At that time the Astros were finally improving, winning more games, but we weren't there yet. I thought we could have had a better ballclub. The main factor was just not scoring enough runs. It was always in the back of my mind when I went to the mound that I might have to pitch a shutout to win. That was a lot of motivation for me to keep improving and keep cutting down on my walks. Giving up a walk was like giving up a hit. I had to get my walks down. It seemed that if you walked that first guy in an inning, he always came around to score. It never failed unless you struck out the next three.

By 1979 I had been in the Astros' organization for 10 years. It had taken me a long time to work my way up from rookie ball to a place on the roster full-time and to become a big winner with respect from all over the sport. There were times I was frustrated with the Astros because I didn't feel I should have been sent back to the minors. There were times I thought I could have been used more. And there were times that I thought the front office could have worked harder to make us a better team.

My first few years in the majors during the first half of the 1970s, I didn't think there was a lot of sincerity among my teammates. There was a lack of closeness. I was a loner by nature but would have liked more camaraderie. To be a complete team, the guys should get together, go out to eat breakfast, lunch, or dinner on the road. That way you get a chance to know a person away from the field and the clubhouse. I think that held the team back a little bit.

My first tendency was to be a loner because I didn't always want to run with the crowd in nightclubs and bars too much. I was afraid of getting into trouble because somebody in the crowd did something that would get all of us arrested and charged. I did make some good friends like Cabell, Bob Watson, Jose Cruz, and guys like that who are still my friends today. What happened was that some guys hung around with certain other guys, and that became a habit. You tended to stay around the same guys all of the time and you never really got close to the rest of your teammates. I wish that had been different.

13

The 1980 Season

If the baseball world thought it had seen it all from J.R. Richard in the late 1970s when he won 74 games in four seasons, won a National League ERA title, and broke the 300-strikeout barrier twice, in 1980 they were about to learn that was all just a warm-up, akin to an orchestra's vamp til ready.

To some degree J.R. had been plagued by slow starts in the spring of each season, whether through his own fault or bad luck. He had always seemed to come on strong in the second half of the season like a charging thoroughbred in the home stretch. But in the 1980 season, he got off to a 100-meter dash man's start, exploding out of the starting blocks.

Richard timed his excellence right for once. He was mesmerizing National League batters, and when the All-Star ballots were counted, J.R's phone rang. Even if the honor seemed overdue, he was a first-time All-Star in 1980. In addition he was anointed his league's starting pitcher by NL manager Chuck Tanner of the Pittsburgh Pirates for the July 8 game at Dodger Stadium.

The American League was managed by the Baltimore Orioles' Earl Weaver, whose starter was his own Steve Stone. The only other Astro selected was Richard's friend, outfielder Jose Cruz, who was also on his first All-Star roster. The NL won the game 4–2, but Richard did not get a decision. He pitched two innings of scoreless ball, allowing one hit.

Meanwhile, the Astros were on the rise. They had rarely experienced good fortune or major successes since their birth as the Colt .45s as an expansion team in 1962. But coming off the 89–73 record of 1979, Houston seemed one player away from being able to make a run at a pennant.

In November of 1979, free-agent, right-handed flamethrower Nolan Ryan, on his way to Hall of Fame enshrinement, became that Astros player. Less than three weeks after hitting the market, he was an Astro. Ryan, a native Texan, wanted to come home after years of pitching for the New York Mets and California Angels. He was a coveted property, even at 33, and he was such a noted fastball hurler that his nickname was the "Ryan Express." The Astros added a premium pitcher to their starting rotation, and the pairing of Ryan and Richard as dual speedball throwers promised endless delight to Astros fans. With knuckleballer Joe Niekro in the mix, and that trio supplemented by Ken Forsch and Vern Ruhle, the Astros were strong top to bottom at the most important position in the sport.

The Astros began the season strongly, but they did not run away with the National League West Division standings. They engaged in a dramatic pennant race all season with the Los Angeles Dodgers and the Cincinnati Reds. Houston prevailed with a record of 93–70, one game ahead of the Dodgers and three-and-a-half games ahead of the Reds. Entering the final weekend of regular-season play, the Astros seemed to be in control of their fate. But the Astros were in

Los Angeles for a three-game series. It was Friday, Saturday, Sunday of October 3, 4, 5. One Houston victory, and the Astros would clinch.

There was only one problem: the Astros couldn't nail down that last win. Friday the Dodgers won 3–2. Saturday the Dodgers won 2–1. Sunday the Dodgers won 4–3. The division crown was slipping away amidst incredible drama. The regular season ended in a tie, and the Astros had to stay in Los Angeles for a playoff game to determine which team would advance to the National League Championship Series to face the Philadelphia Phillies, champions of the East Division.

It took four days and four games of a seemingly interminable weekend for Houston to clinch, but they wiped out the Dodgers in the Monday playoff 7–1. It was as if the Astros had saved all of their clutch hits for the emergency game. Niekro notched the win, his 20th of the season. It was Niekro's second straight 20-win campaign for Houston. He was one of a limited number of knuckleball specialists in baseball history to win 20 games in a season.

Richard built a strong All-Star resume during the first months of the 1980 season. At the All-Star break, his record was 10–4, a .714 winning percentage. His ERA was a spectacular 1.96 at the time. He averaged more than a strikeout an inning. J.R. was in the midst of the best season of his career, certainly on pace to win 20 games again, lead the league in strikeouts again, and probably capture a second ERA title. "He had probably reached a peak," said Astros pitcher Larry Dierker. "He was so good it was hard to imagine him getting better. I suppose it was possible. During those last couple of years, he was probably going as well as anyone ever—Sandy Koufax, Pedro Martinez. It's reasonable to assume that he would have been able to do it at that rate for another six or seven years."

Something that impressed Dierker about Richard's pitching at that point in his career beyond his blinding fastball was how much control he had gained over his slider. "He was probably throwing 93 mph with his slider," Dierker said. "Most guys' broke six to 12 inches. His broke a couple of feet. It had so much movement."

Catcher Johnny Edwards, Richard's favorite receiver with the Astros, said it was tough to tell just how fast J.R. threw because radar guns were not in use the whole time he was pitching and may not have been as accurate as they are now. It wasn't always easy to catch Richard either. But Edwards was another fan of the fastball-slider combo. "For sure he was in the high 90s," Edwards said of J.R.'s speed. "At times he was in the 100s. He could work me over pretty good. The slider, that was his other pitch. The slider was wicked. They would just eat me alive, trying to knock them down." Edwards said when Richard was at his best during the 1970s, "right-handed batters were afraid of him. Willie Mays told me to tell J.R. to just keep the ball away from him."

Cruz was one of Richard's best friends on the Astros in the clubhouse and away from it. They fished together in their free time. They ate breakfast together on road trips. Cruz was always glad that J.R. was on his team so he did not have to hit against him in games that counted in the standings. That would have been a nightmare, he said. "He was the most intimidating guy," Cruz said. "Not too many people in baseball wanted to face J.R. Richard. He threw hard and he was a big man with long arms. Off the field he was like a kid. We used to joke around like brothers."

Cruz said it was something for Houston to have Richard and Ryan in the same rotation, both with arms that threw pitches which broke the speed limit. "It was impressive," Cruz said, "to have two guys throwing 100 mph. To me, when I had J.R. on my side pitching, I felt great, like we were going to win."

In 1980 that's what the Astros did most of the time. J.R. Richard was receiving more attention from the national press and baseball fans than ever before. He was on pace for a brilliant season and he was primed for the second half of the season following his All-Star debut. He never could have imagined what lurked over the horizon for him, how his life was about to change dramatically in unforeseen ways.

J.R. Richard

Boy, playing the first few months of that season was fun. The team was doing well, we were battling for first place, and we had Nolan Ryan and Joe Niekro and me pitching well. Nolan is a great guy, a great guy. I can't take anything away from him. What I hate and regret is that during those months we were together on the Astros that we did not communicate more. He probably could have taught me more about pitching, about the hitters, and vice versa. I could have given him some insight into the National League hitters and pitchers because he had been in the American League for a while. We were both power pitchers. He could have given me some insight, wisdom, and knowledge about setting up hitters because most of what I learned I learned the hard way. We just didn't talk as much as we should have. I think we just mostly hung out with different guys.

Nolan won 11 games for the Astros that year with a 3.35 ERA, just a tiny piece of his career. He won 327 games and struck out more men than anyone else in history. I threw faster than he did. No doubt about it. No doubt about it in my mind. I didn't worry about who threw faster. When a new guy came to the team, I was more concerned with personalities, and he was the type of guy who you would always want as a friend.

If Nolan and I were similar as pitchers, then Joe Niekro was a completely different animal. He was an amazing guy with his knuckleball. He could throw that knuckler and make it dance. I would watch him and say, "Man, that's unbelievable." I was watching the game on TV the time when the umpires nailed

133

him for having an emery board in his pocket. Everybody said that Mike Scott was scuffing the ball on his belt buckle or something. If you want to scuff the ball, it's easy to do. You've got a catcher, a first baseman, anyone in the infield can help you when they throw the ball around. To make the ball just drop out of sight like he did, that's unbelievable. I've thrown a knuckler and I have never seen a ball drop out of the sky the way Scott's did. There was something wrong with that ball. I couldn't even scratch it and make the ball do what he did.

Niekro was a good guy. We both had the same job description. We were both pitchers. But I threw 100 mph, and he threw 65 mph or something. We used to tease one another. He'd say to me, "Watch this heater. Watch this heater." Then he threw his fastball, and I would look at him with a straight face and say, "Man, that's some smoke. You're not taking any speed away from me, are you?" He was a good guy, too. It was a shame when he passed away. I tried to make him feel good about how fast he was throwing the ball even if we were joking.

I had tried to become a success in the majors for a long time, and when I did it, that was very gratifying. I was at the peak of my pitching in 1980 and I thought I would still get better. But no matter how you measure it, I was a success. I won 20 games. I made the All-Star team. I struck out more than 300 batters in a season twice.

Becoming successful taught me a lot. It taught me a lot about human behavior. It taught me to make sure I was respectful of all people. I was making a lot of money for the time in baseball and I realized God was giving me a lot of money, but it was not all for me. He gives you money to share with other people. If God blesses you, you're supposed to bless other people and that's what I did. One thing I did was help the homeless.

The most amount of money I made playing in the majors was $850,000. That is a lot of money by everyday American standards. It is not that much compared to current baseball salaries. The minimum salary for the last guy on the bench, the 25th man, is more than $500,000, so an awful lot of guys make more than $1 million a year. But by any standard, $850,000 is a good living.

I gave homeless people money. I took homeless people out to eat with me sometimes. Sometimes they couldn't get into places because they needed a bath. I gave some people money to help them, and some people screwed me, but I didn't know any better when I gave the wrong people money. With the homeless I wanted to be kind and I felt I had to give back and help them. With my family I intended to give certain relatives loans, but I found out you can't lend money to family. Give them money if you can afford it but don't lend them money. Once it's done, it's done, and you can't go back. The past is past. You cannot live in the past. You've got to keep your eyes on the future. My family was happy for me, and family members were proud of me. My siblings looked up to me, but they never came to Houston to go to games. They could have had free tickets at any time, but they didn't come to watch me pitch. That always surprised me. I don't know why in the world that was. It isn't that far from Ruston, Louisiana, to Houston, Texas. They just didn't show up.

By 1980 I was a big star in Houston. My wife and I went out on the town together. Although I didn't make very many public appearances, I got recognized all of the time, everywhere I went. I was living full-time, year-round in Houston after I got married. The only time I wasn't living in Houston was when the Astros went to spring training.

The great thing was never having arm problems. I didn't miss starts. My main task to build my stamina was to run all of the time, keep my legs in shape. I took care of them. For most fans the clubhouse is a mysterious place, but to me it was the place where I prepared to play. When it was my turn to pitch, I didn't fool around or joke around. I sat in front of my locker getting ready. I put earphones on and listened to music. I'd get myself so pumped up. I was so ready that all I needed was about three warm-up pitches.

On the days I wasn't pitching, the clubhouse could be a lot of fun. Everyone made a big deal about it when Joe Pepitone started using a hair dryer. He was the first guy in baseball, and some people made fun of him because they thought it was too girly. One day we put a bunch of baby powder into Pepitone's hair dryer. He turned the hair dryer on and, of course, he came out looking like Buckwheat—only white.

We used to play all kinds of practical jokes in the clubhouse. We used to put the hot ointment that was rubbed into muscles into the seat of a guy's underwear. He would get dressed and during a game you would see him twist and squirm on the bench in the dugout, and we would bust our sides laughing. We played all kinds of stupid games in the clubhouse. The craziest guy was Doug Rader. He was a nut, man. He sat on a birthday cake nude once. He would pull your pants down in the dugout. He definitely kept things loose, though sometimes he could take it too far. Sometimes he would hit a golf ball in the clubhouse. That could be dangerous, but since nobody got hurt, he thought it was funny. Since he was hitting .365, maybe people might think anything was funny.

As much as I loved striking out people and the adrenaline boost I got from it, I think the fans liked it even more. They got more pleasure out of it than I did based on the way they responded. Fans react much more strongly to a strikeout than a ground ball out. One thing I don't remember back then is them having any of the sports memorabilia shows where they paid you to come and sign autographs. I didn't make appearances. I didn't have any endorsements. The marketing world sure has changed and grown since I played. There might have been some endorsement opportunities for some guys, but it was not like it is today.

When Michael Jordan came along and everyone wanted to sponsor him, I think that was a breakthrough in marketing, and it led to opportunities for other athletes. Then along came Tiger Woods. Jordan and Tiger made more money from endorsements than from salary or winnings. It was a different time when I was playing. Maybe if you had a real savvy agent who could understand the marketplace, you might have gotten a piece of the pie. Now the marketing of pro athletes is unbelievable. It's everywhere.

When the 1980 season began, I was setting them up and knocking them down. It was a super fast start, the reverse of my other seasons. I picked it up from the second half of my 1979 season and improved from there. I thought I might win 25 games that year and definitely go over 300 strikeouts again. I was on a roll that season. My confidence was growing by leaps and bounds. I just felt as if I couldn't lose. I was rolling like a snowball going downhill.

I was chosen for my first All-Star team. *Finally.* Getting the start was a thrill, and the American League had so many great players. They had Rod Carew, Carlton Fisk, and Reggie

Jackson. That's three Hall of Famers in the starting lineup. What a powerful hitter Jackson was. It was so enjoyable to be in that position. I went out there thinking, *This game is mine*, even though I knew I wouldn't pitch long because it was an All-Star Game. I was totally focused. I put on a new hat and put it on just right. I figured the opposition couldn't touch me.

In my two innings, I struck out Reggie, Fisk and their pitcher, Steve Stone. Johnny Bench was my catcher and he dropped a lot of my pitches, even though he was definitely a great catcher. I mowed the batters down at the knees. Pitching in the All-Star Game was a definite high point for me. That meant I was in the best company in the game. After the game ended with a National League win, we all rejoined our teams for the second half of the season. I had every reason to believe that I was in the middle of my best season and that the second half held great things in store for me.

There was no clue as to what was coming for me. I was 30 years old, in my prime, pitching as well as anyone in the majors. If you had told me that my appearance in the All-Star Game was going to be the next to last game I ever pitched in the big leagues, I would not have believed you. It was unfathomable. But soon after I hooked back up with the Astros, my life changed forever.

14

Launching a Comeback

The news that J.R. Richard had suffered from a blood clot and a stroke and was dealing with the aftermath of those serious health issues stunned baseball fans and sent sportswriters into a frenzy of writing and reporting. Big, strong, powerful J.R. was laid up in bed, still seriously ill, removed from the Houston Astros, and facing very real problems that indicated he would not pitch again soon and that his return to life as a professional athlete was uncertain. But from the beginning, he was determined on making a comeback doctors said couldn't be done.

Richard's wife, Carolyn, flew to Houston from Louisiana, leaving the couple's five children there, before doctors operated on her husband. At the same time that J.R. was undergoing surgery, the Astros played a game against the Philadelphia Phillies and lost 6–4. Neither Bill Virdon nor his coaching staff and the players knew about Richard's emergency surgery before the game. "We didn't find out about the operation until after the game had started," Virdon said.

"Until then, the players hadn't been too concerned, but that got them to thinking. At least it will put an end to all the speculation. You don't replace a pitcher like J.R., but if there's one area where we could stand any loss, it's pitching. We'll go with a four-man rotation of [Nolan] Ryan, Ken Forsch, Joe Niekro, and Vern Ruhle. We're more concerned with J.R.s health right now."

There had been considerable media speculation about what was wrong with Richard—if anything—and there had been doubters who criticized him. Anyone who had written anything negative about Richard had to swiftly backpedal. It was all difficult to believe, a prominent athlete, only weeks removed from an All-Star Game appearance, being leveled like this. People scrambled for explanations, but there were none forthcoming that were satisfactory. There was some angry backlash from teammates who wondered if slow response and reaction to Richard's health complaints stemmed from racism. Third baseman Enos Cabell, an African American, raised the issue. "If 'J' were white, maybe they would have checked him more thoroughly and maybe he wouldn't have been out there throwing," Cabell said. "Most black athletes play hurt, and he pitched when he was hurt."

From a baseball standpoint, especially in Houston, many fans wondered if this spelled a death knell to the Astros' chances of finishing in first place in their division. Team officials, players, and fans hung on doctor reports, which generally were pretty vague. Some reports came from team officials, and the public statements were not terribly encouraging. One cited doctors' analysis of Richard's condition, saying, "It must be recognized that there is a possibility that there may be residual weakness involving his left arm and left leg. The doctors state that it is not completely predictable at the present time."

Most Americans either have a loved one who suffered a stroke, a friend who dealt with one, or have read about them. The long-term residual effects are indeed unpredictable, but they know sometimes there can be speech impairment, memory loss, diminished muscle function, and possible difficulty walking if one side of the body has been particularly impacted. Almost certainly, in none of those cases, however, had the loved one or friend been a professional athlete with a finely honed physique. J.R. was probably the entirety of his own sample. It was so challenging to become a professional athlete for a living, necessitating all of one's mental acumen and physical skills that any lessening of full strength would likely put the future in jeopardy.

Astros owner John McMullen issued a statement regarding Richard's health. "There is no fear for his life," McMullen said. "But now there is some fear for his life as an athlete." Astros officials were initially informed by doctors that Richard might be able to resume playing with the team within four weeks, but an update of his condition 12 hours after surgery revealed the numbness on the left side. Doctors said that the weakness could pass quickly, but it was too soon to be sure. "It does raise questions that weren't there last night when we were told he might be back with the team in a month," McMullen added. "This could prolong his recovery. They just don't know."

Once the seriousness of Richard's condition became known, there were almost daily news bulletins issued as status reports, measuring his improvement and speculating on whether or not he would be able to rejoin the Astros and return to top-shelf performance. The two matters were inextricably linked. Doctors talked to the Astros, and the Astros issued public statements. Newspapers all over the country and the Associated Press and United Press International wire services kept on top of the story. They tried to report any single word of encouragement if J.R. moved even one toe on his left foot. "His condition has been upgraded from stable to improved," said Houston public relations spokesman Rick Rivers.

Doctors said J.R. had gained strength on his left side, and if his arm and leg returned to normal, then he would be able to pitch again. Certainly that's how Richard's father James Clayton received the news, interpreting a report he received from Lamar, one of J.R's brothers. One thing the elder Richard made clear two days after J.R.'s collapse in the Astrodome was: "J.R. won't pitch again this year."

Whether the sportswriters thought they were being clever, or it was merely inevitable, stories about J.R. Richard, the pitcher, which had previously deemed his condition "mysterious" tied his situation to the popular TV show *Dallas* and its main character J.R. Ewing, who was coping with his own mysterious problems. In the follow-up to Richard's collapse and surgery, some writers tried to piece together the entire saga of Richard's illness.

At one point Richard admitted that Dr. Frank Jobe in Los Angeles had not told him to sit out 30 days, but he just felt like saying that. He did have a stomachache when he left the game early against the Atlanta Braves probably because of a hamburger he ate not agreeing with him, but it was not the reason behind his departure. Not seeing the catcher clearly and feeling as if he had a dead arm were more compelling reasons to leave the game so early.

Houston general manager Tal Smith and manager Virdon both thought the impact of the first arm problems of his life caused Richard to make some of the statements he was issuing. When J.R. actually went onto the disabled list, he stopped talking to reporters, saying, "I've been saying too much."

Soon, none of that would matter. The overriding issues were Richard's collapse, stroke, blood clot, surgery, and prognosis. Some thoughtful writers began examining the step-by-step actions taken and not taken after J.R. first said he didn't feel right. Some concluded that he was treated shabbily and that more attention should have been paid to his complaints. A story from the Field News Service was headlined, "Was J.R. done wrong?"

A few days after Richard's Astrodome collapse, his surgery, and diagnosis, writer Michael Madden said, "The stroke was major, the doctors now finally say, and so is the controversy. And it is a Texas-sized controversy where blame is being aimed at the Astros, medical science, doctors, the effects of throwing the slider on a pitcher's arm, and the press. There must be some way to explain the inexplicable, to explain why a baseball pitcher in the prime of his life should have collapsed in a heap in the outfield of the Astrodome while going through light drills. Or perhaps there is no explanation at all."

Jim Murray, the famous Los Angeles Times sports columnist who later won a Pulitzer Prize, also discussed whether J.R. might have been a victim of the locker-room warrior syndrome that says you play if you can walk. "You look at James Rodney Richard, and it's preposterous to think of him in terms of fever charts, encephalograms, blood clots, thromboses, aneurysms or—for crying out loud—strokes," Murray wrote. "Strokes and electrocardiograms are for middle-aged men with paunches and bifocals, not ballplayers. Ballplayers have sore arms, pulled hamstrings, calf muscle pulls—macho injuries like that. The occasional toothache. Stuff you can fix with a cast, or a crutch, or a drill. Or just rub a little dirt on it and go back out there. Or get called 'Puss.'" Murray sarcastically scored those who didn't think Richard's complaints about dizziness and the like were significant. "One more nine-inning game and not only would his arm be dead, so would J.R.," Murray said.

After his initial blush of anger and his suggestion of racism, Cabell backed off his earlier statements and made some more thoughtful comments that cut across skin color lines. "I guess it makes everybody say, 'Do we judge people too much?'" Cabell said. "A lot of people crucified J.R. when they didn't even know the man." Cabell said that Richard did misspeak to reporters when he told them Jobe had sidelined him for 30 days. But Cabell said the reason was, "He just got tired of them writing stuff and said the first thing that popped in his mind."

Cabell said Richard was "killing the weights" in workouts during the offseason, calling him "Hercules," and Richard's sheer athleticism, power pitching, and strength fooled people into believing he had to be healthy. "People didn't know how a man like that could be hurting."

J.R. Richard

Before I was rushed to the hospital, I went through all kinds of tests and examinations and was told no surgery was needed. Then I was sent back to the Astros and told I could do light workouts. That didn't make it sound as if I was facing any serious health problem. When I collapsed and was lying on the field at the Astrodome I was thinking, *Why do some people have a doctor's license?*

The only worry I really had at that point was not knowing what was wrong with me. I was in good shape, felt pretty good overall, and everything was going great on the mound. It wasn't until I was in the hospital and came out of surgery that I heard the word "stroke." Eventually someone wrote a report that after all of the CAT scans the doctors said I had three strokes, three little strokes. Then a doctor said one was major. There was a lot of different talk going on at the time, making it difficult to tell what was really happening.

When the doctors started talking to me about having a stroke, I wasn't 100 percent sure what it was. I knew that it could kill me. They, though, didn't tell me that. I found that out afterward. They didn't tell me too much of anything in the beginning. I was recovering from surgery and I had the numbness on the left side. That worried me.

I don't remember the doctors mentioning anything to me about pitching again. They weren't saying much of anything. My father came from Louisiana, and he was praying out loud. At that time I was incapacitated. I couldn't talk at first. I couldn't really hear well. I was totally paralyzed on my left side. Even now, all of these years later, when it's hot and humid out I sweat like crazy on my right side and I am as dry as powder on my left side. I heard that the doctors cut out my sweat glands on the left side. I guess they cut the nerves. So I don't sweat on that side. When I was in that hospital bed, I was pretty much out of it.

It was obvious to me that I wasn't going to be pitching again that season. I was determined to pitch again, though. The Astros hung in there and won the National League West Division. They won 93 games and advanced to the National League Championship Series and played the Philadelphia Phillies. The Phillies were very good that year. They had Steve Carlton and Pete Rose and a lot of good guys. They beat the Astros three games to two and went on to the World Series. They won it, too.

Everybody said the playoff was one of the best series ever and they said, "We know if you'd been there, we'd have won it." You really never know about those things. You'd like to think you could have made a difference. I know I would have pitched against the Dodgers at the end of the regular season when it came down to a one-game playoff and I would have pitched against the Phillies. I got the feeling that people didn't care a hoot about you—only what you could do.

After I got out of the hospital, my first task was to go through rehab to build myself up again, especially on the left side. Baseball was being played, and all I could do was watch on TV. I missed the rest of that season, the last couple of months. It was a slow process to rebuild my strength in my muscles, my hand-eye coordination. I was depressed, though mostly because I hated the rehab.

One thing the therapists had me do was put matches into different holes and then pins into different holes. They were working on my fine motor skills. The idea was to do small things, handle delicate things, so I could work my fingers and work my thumb. I had to pick things up with my left hand because that was the side that had been paralyzed. Over and over again, I had to do things of that nature. I hated doing it.

It's like you have to learn to do things all over again as if you are a baby or a little kid learning for the first time. It was very tedious to do the baby things over and over. The repetition got to me, using my left hand to do this and do that again and again and again. I used to dread it. Finally, I got used to it and realized I've got to do this. I was still weaker on my left side, but I could see a little bit of improvement. Eventually, I started to enjoy it. We worked my left hand very hard. They demanded I do all of these things with my left side. But even today I still find it difficult sometimes to do things with my left hand, arm, and side. If I catch something on the left side, I do it with my left arm up against my chest. So I'm still affected by the stroke.

I suppose I will still have some effects from the stroke for the rest of my days. Yet at the same time, I am not as bad off as some other people who have had strokes and who could not bounce back as far as I did. I feel that I am very fortunate that the rehabilitation helped me as much as it did. I am not going to say lucky. I'll say I am blessed because I was able to come back. I have to say I might have been a little bit spoiled at the time. I was a baseball star. I was a celebrity. I was making a lot of money. People gave me free things because I was a player for the Houston Astros. I was on top of the world. Beautiful girls came up to me and threw themselves at me, saying, "I love you." I turned them down because I was married, but the lifestyle had just been handed to me.

A stroke was the last thing I was thinking of happening to me. *Why would I?* Everything was just clicking. I would go out there to the mound and throw nine innings as if it was a walk in the park. Then suddenly, I am sidelined. I am hospitalized. Instead of being with my teammates for the rest of the 1980 season and leading them into the playoffs, I am doing rehab every day, tediously doing rehab. It was a slow recovery.

Given what happened to me it was inevitable that I would think, *Why me?* I was very depressed during the rest of the season when I got home. I started gaining weight. I bought a lot of beer and I sat around on the couch eating hot pork skins. I'd eat those and drink beer and be depressed. It was not exactly a good, healthy diet. I wanted to exercise and try to start getting back in shape, but I couldn't run. I went outside and tried to run, and my wind was cut. I couldn't do anything. It was just total fatigue. No matter what I did for exercise, it didn't work. I wasn't strong enough. I'd become fatigued and out of breath right away. I got to the point where I quit trying to work out and just sat around and gained weight.

A lot of the feeling came back on my left side, but I was still very weak all around. I had always been an athlete with almost no body fat and I had been in shape my whole life. Now I had to start over completely and I didn't have the strength to do it at first. That was very discouraging. I fought through some of the depression and told myself that I was going to pitch again.

I was determined to do it. I made my mind up. I pushed myself to exercise and start my conditioning. I wanted to do a little and then increase, but I just couldn't do much for a while. After months the most I could do was run a mile. That's all.

There was no way I was going to be strong enough to pitch for the Astros in 1981. People concluded that I was all finished. I had recovered a lot of movement from the stroke, but I hadn't recovered the abilities that made me an athlete. It was a hard time. Then things got worse on the personal front. It seemed as soon as I was out of the hospital and out of baseball, my wife Carolyn, divorced me. You know how she divorced me? She was fixing breakfast for the kids, who were going to school. I was in bed asleep and I heard somebody at the door. She went to open the door and she yelled that somebody was there for me so I got up. I went to the front door, and it was a policeman serving me with divorce papers. I just took the papers, went back to the room, and went back to sleep.

Every improvement in my health came from a lot of physical work. I had never been scared of working hard to improve my physical strength, but the difference then was that I was coming from a totally different level. Instead of being a professional athlete who wanted to get better, I was a regular person who had been struck down by illness and I had a long, long way to go to rebuild the strength I had before.

Coming back to being a major leaguer meant a lot to me, and I put in day after day of workouts. By the spring of 1981, I thought I was ready to give it a try to return to the Astros. It had only been six months, but it was a new baseball season, and I didn't want it to start without me. I wanted to get back to the Astros and back to the majors.

15

Throwing Out the First Pitch

The ordeal of J.R. Richard was not a short one. The stroke was so devastating to his system that even careful surgery could not cure the entire problem all at once. Most people found the circumstances unbelievable. Richard's stature seemed to offer no evidence that he could be felled by such an unusual development. But once that was digested, it also became apparent that regaining full strength was going to be an ongoing battle as well. Once word spread that Richard was experiencing long-lasting aftereffects that hindered his mobility, it was assumed that he would never pitch in the big leagues again.

Richard did not admit that—nor did he believe that. Athletes' will is sometimes as powerful as their speed and strength, the attributes that set them apart from the average person. Richard had a strong will and belief in his capabilities. In the weeks after his 1980 baseball season ended and he began the steps to recovery, he never let his thoughts waver about a comeback.

Teammates and other players could not fathom Richard's condition. In their frame of reference, strokes afflicted the elderly—not 30-year-old athletes. Houston pitching coach Mel Wright said he had never encountered anything like the series of events, which struck Richard. Doctors, coaches, and players re-examined their thought processes dating back to when J.R. first complained of feeling poorly. Some players may have felt guilty for doubting Richard's veracity, but doctors refused to second-guess their testing publicly. At the very least, they were being careful not to admit mistakes just in case Richard wanted to sue them for malpractice.

As more information became known and was interpreted, sportswriters became bolder in their statements. Although his pitching career might well be jeopardized, the consensus of stories indicated it was very likely that the emergency surgery saved Richard's life. Dr. Harold Brelsford, Houston's team doctor and the point man for many of the statements issued, was closely monitoring J.R.s health in the hospital and made no hasty public assessments saying Richard would never pitch again. His words seemed to hold out hope for a pitching comeback.

"It all depends on how much damage was done to his central nervous system," Brelsford said. Brelsford said that after looking at Richard's physical condition post-surgery he had "guarded optimism" that he might attain a complete recovery.

Richard resented the fact that doctors who had given him a battery of tests in Houston prior to the stroke seemed to have missed warning signs. Brelsford defended the test results that allowed Richard to leave the hospital and resume light workouts of the type he was performing when he collapsed on the Astrodome field. "[It had] all the experts baffled," Brelsford said. "His neck arteries had been thoroughly checked the previous week, and they were fine then. The clot in his neck had to happen between the time the tests were performed and the following Wednesday." Richard has always been skeptical of that description and thinks doctors missed something. "One of two things apparently had to happen," Brelsford said. "One, a clot would have had to proceed from the shoulder to the neck, and clots don't do that, or at least nobody in the department at Methodist Hospital has known it to happen, or the second possibility is he picked up an embolus from the heart. If that's the case, then this is completely unrelated to anything that happened before." Like most laymen—Richard—had a difficult time digesting that explanation of coincidence. Brelsford insisted that Richard "had the best medical treatment in the world."

In a case that some hoped would parallel J.R.'s and offer optimism for recovery, a St. Louis reporter conversed with St. Louis Cardinals pitcher Bob Sykes not long after Richard was hospitalized. When Sykes was with the Detroit Tigers in 1977, he similarly experienced a tired arm and was diagnosed with a blood clot in his shoulder. The clot vanished on its own in the offseason. This is what Richard's doctors thought would happen when they sent him home after his tests, albeit with restrictions on the difficulty of his workouts.

Sykes' blood clot, however, reappeared in 1979 after he had joined the Cardinals. Sykes was pitching in a game and he worried about the absence of feeling in his left throwing arm. He also experienced the same kind of fatigue J.R. noted when he had to be lifted from games earlier instead of being capable of pitching into the late innings. At a St. Louis hospital, doctors discovered that a piece of muscle in Sykes' arm had grown over an artery, hampering circulation. Sykes missed two months of play after undergoing a surgical procedure. He did come back and pitch for the Cardinals in 1980 and 1981 before his career ended. Sykes won 23 games lifetime.

Weeks after Richard's hospitalization, Sykes said he had been suspicious of what ailed Richard after hearing of his dead arm complaints. He wondered if J.R.'s problem could have been the same as his. Sykes also predicted that if he could come back, then J.R. could come back. "My best goes out to J.R.," Sykes said. "But I did it. I know he can do it. He's stronger than I am."

The more information that became known about Richard's condition and the denouement of the stroke, more athletes stepped forward in support. There had originally been some grumbling in Houston when Richard skipped turns in the rotation. Some could not understand the problem since Richard possessed an arm that was still producing magical numbers. Were pennant chances being jeopardized for nothing? An anonymous Astro said, "We're in the pennant race, and he pulls this?" No reported follow-up quotes were attributed to that player after Richard dropped to the floor of the Astrodome from his illness. "They didn't believe J.R. because they didn't want to," said Baltimore Orioles pitcher Jim Palmer, a future Hall of Famer, who said the same thing happened to him. "They don't want you hurt. They're in a pennant race, and he's their top pitcher."

Reggie Smith, a seven-time All-Star outfielder, said the emphasis on playing hurt is ingrained in athletes starting in junior high school and it is no different in the major leagues.

"The thing I've found over the years," Smith said, "the nature of the game itself is that the people who are 'in control of the game,' say if you don't play hurt, you're a sissy. It goes back to junior high. You always get up. If you're knocked down, it's 'Get up, you're not hurt that bad, you're still breathing.' So you did get up. You got up because you didn't know any better."

Once Richard was out of the hospital and completed a rehab regimen, he was basically on his own in terms of taking physical steps toward a baseball comeback. Although Richard was a bit shaky when he did so, J.R. threw out the first pitch when the Astros hosted a home playoff game. It was pretty much his first pitch in some time, too.

Richard wasn't finished with doctors yet, though, and in October Richard returned to the hospital for more surgery. This time an 18-hour operation involved transplanting an eight-inch piece of artery from his stomach into his right shoulder. It was felt that was something that might facilitate speed in regaining strength there.

During the Christmas season, Richard was well enough to resume some of his old hobbies, trekking through the Texas backwoods hunting rabbits with rifle and dog. Richard's speech had been slurred by the stroke, but gradually, steadily, that improved, as well. First pitch aside, Richard's body told him enough about how far he had to go to be a big league pitcher once more. "I'm at the bottom of the mountain," he said around Christmas of 1980. "Now I have to start climbing to the top. There's no doubt in my mind that I'll be back. I feel terrific."

Richard, like many people who have close calls, re-examined his life and recognized how lucky he was for the athletic achievements he had earned and the things baseball had given him. But he also recognized one thing was more precious than those experiences. "My gift for Christmas is being alive," he said.

Even as he was checking out of the hospital following the October surgery, Richard made a pledge to a doctor who asked what he was going to do. Richard said the first thing he was going to do was go fishing. Then, as his strength returned, he said, "Going to pitch."

Despite his great determination and labors over the winter and in spring training of 1981, Richard did not show enough of the right stuff to play ball at the highest competitive level that soon. However, on September 1, 1981, when rosters were expanded for the tail end of the major league season, the Astros activated Richard. That was a bizarre season in baseball, with games lost to a labor action in the middle of the year. Those hostilities resulted in a split season with teams playing around 110 of 162 scheduled games. General manager Al Rosen said he thought Richard's presence in the dugout would be a boost to team morale and Richard's morale as the Astros fought for the right to compete in a playoff after the second half of the season. "We just felt it would be a psychological uplift to J.R.," Rosen said. "He's worked awfully hard to get back to where he is, and we would be remiss if we didn't show him our appreciation. We wanted him to be part of it, and the ballclub felt the same way."

Richard passed a variety of agility tests, looked good in selected drills, and had thrown on the sidelines with regular Houston catcher Alan Ashby. "He's throwing the ball well, and his velocity is good," Ashby said. "Frankly, I don't think he'd even stand here and tell you his control was real sharp. But I think everyone's astounded at his recovery."

Fellow pitcher Joe Niekro also said he thought Richard was looking good and he wanted to see him out there in a game. However, no promise was made to J.R. that he would actually pitch in one of the season's remaining contests, Rosen said. That would be up to manager Bill Virdon, who said that Richard could pitch if "the circumstances were right." But Richard never got into a game, and later Virdon said he did not feel J.R. had regained the necessary crispness to play.

Richard did not give up. In 1982 he continued to compete for a spot on the Astros roster and went back to the minors to regain his game form. At age 32, long after his last showing in the Florida State League, J.R. returned to Class A competition. He pitched in six games for Daytona Beach, went 3–1, and recorded a 2.79 ERA. Then he was promoted to Triple A Tucson. That did not go as well. Richard made six appearances, finished 0–2, and his ERA was an unsightly 13.68. Richard's strikeouts also were down. At Daytona Beach he fanned 28 men in 42 innings. At Tucson he struck out 13 batters in 24⅓ innings.

J.R. Richard

No matter what happens, life carries on. The clock never stops ticking. My life changed suddenly and in several ways. My health had been affected. I was no longer a major league pitcher and I split up with my wife.

I didn't react strongly when my wife filed for divorce. I think I was still in depression mode. I just kind of said, "Okay, if that's what you want." I was just going through the motions in life for a while. She took the kids, and I lost $700,000 in the divorce.

After a while, when I had the energy, I started looking for jobs to support myself. I used to work at a place called A-One Mobile Homes and after work I sometimes went over to a club on South Main Street. It was like an after-five-o'clock hangout. They sold coffee, and at that time, I became a coffee fanatic. So every day after work, I stopped in there and drank coffee, coffee, coffee. A guy I knew in there knew a football player, and he introduced me to a woman who used to be a cheerleader for the Houston Oilers. That was before the Oilers moved to Nashville and were replaced by the Houston Texans.

She became my second wife. Her name was Zemphry, and she was working at the post office when we met. She was no longer a cheerleader by then. I married her on the rebound when I was at a low point. We were only married for a few years. I caught her going through my mail, and she refused to give me an investment check I had. That's when I said, "Oh, no, it's time." That was the end of our relationship.

Throughout the early 1980s after my stroke, I refused to believe that I wouldn't wind up pitching for the Astros again. I worked hard at my conditioning and training after my body started to come back. I did a lot of training with the Texas Southern University baseball team in 1981. That led me back to the Astros. When I got stronger over the summer, I pitched some simulated games for Houston, and they put me back on the team starting September 1 when the rosters expanded. Big league teams have roster limits of 25 for most of the season, but in September they are allowed to expand by quite a few guys. Mostly they bring up guys from Triple A who had good seasons. If they are young guys, the team wants to see what they do in the majors for the first time. Other guys get rewarded. In my case it was more or less a unique thing where it was a reward for everything I had done for the team in the past.

I still had a positive attitude. I was back with the team and I felt I could pitch. But unfortunately it didn't happen. I was with the Astros, but I never got into a game. I thought there would have been a chance to use me at least once. A lot of people thought I should just accept the fact that I was never going to play again. But that wasn't me. I never did accept the fact that I wasn't going to play anymore. I always thought I would be able to. At that time the Astros pretty much said, "Okay, we gave him another shot to play. He just didn't recover in that time."

When they put me on the big league roster, I thought the only thing I had to do was get a chance to play and I would have shown something. I had to prove things to myself and others. I thought it was exceptional that I had made it back that far. I was a guy that had a traumatic stroke, and the doctors almost wanted to cut off my arm. Just to be there was something.

In the beginning, when I first threw after the stroke, I was pretty much just dicking around. I had to get stronger. When I threw out that first pitch in October, that was not the real J.R. During that September back with the Astros, I didn't expect to get a start and a chance to throw a complete game, but I thought I could have pitched in a real game, maybe an inning or two of relief.

It would have meant so much for me to get into another game after the stroke. It would have meant a great deal. It practically would have been a movie. Even if I just went out and pitched an inning, it would have been great. What a feeling that would have been to get out there again in an Astros uniform and play in an official game. I know I could have pitched a couple of innings. But they never called my name that month of September, at least not loud enough for me to hear.

But after September of 1981, I thought I could make it back in 1982. I went to the Florida State League, starting at the bottom of the minors again. I was stronger still and ready to pitch in real games, though those real games were at a level way below the majors. That was the real deal at least. I discovered I had to learn how to pitch all over again. Things didn't come back naturally without work. I did well in Florida, but I was not up to par in Tucson. I got beat up pretty good there. I was throwing 90 mph—not 100 mph—and I didn't feel like the normal me. I didn't have the normal J.R. stamina or attitude. I had a different perception of myself, of who I used to be and who I was then. I wasn't feeling the confidence I used to feel.

My illness had taken a lot of out of me, and I thought about that. I believed I was on track time-wise with the arrival of another baseball season, but evidently I wasn't on my own time plan anymore. I was on the Astros' time frame, someone else's time frame. I didn't have all the time in the world to get ready. You've got to realize—and this is something I realized then—that baseball is a business. I don't care how much they say they love you. If something happens, the team is going to throw you to the wayside. They'll throw you in the ditch, pick up someone else, and keep on rolling.

That summer I was trying to follow all of the steps of moving up through the minor league chain all over again. I wasn't there yet. My slider wasn't as sharp, my fastball wasn't as fast. It kind of got exposed in Triple A. So my comeback stalled out in 1982 in Tucson. Again during the offseason, there were a lot of people telling me to give up and realize I would never pitch in the majors again, but I refused to quit. In the spring of 1983, I returned to baseball again. This time the Astros sent me to their rookie club in the Gulf Coast League. That was full circle from 1969. Almost 15 years later, I was back in rookie ball, playing a two-month season from the end of June until the end of August.

My record was 2–3 with a 3.18 ERA. I started nine games and pitched 51 innings with 46 strikeouts. One thing that happened that year, something I barely remember, is that season kind of got ruined because I began having pain in my left leg. The doctors seemed to think it was a leftover thing from the original stroke and surgery. That interrupted things. I thought I was coming back to my former status, too, slowly but surely. That didn't help me.

I don't think I ever completely regained my full pitching status. I think I would have with time. It was touch and go. It was hard to tell how much time I needed. It was something I had to feel. When my body got back to full strength, I would know it and I would know I had all of my pitching tools again. I was not that old. During the 1983 season, I was only 33.

Part of me refused to acknowledge what the stroke had done to me. If you have a stroke—and the doctors said I had a massive stroke—you become very weak. You stay weak for a long time. Your muscles have to be replenished. Your nerves, your arteries, your muscles, have to be replenished. It's a life-threatening illness. They said the main problem was a massive stroke, but there was the blood clot, and I believe two other smaller strokes in there. I am very fortunate to be alive.

After all of that, I felt the pitching comeback was right there. I pitched well in the Florida State League and then got hit hard in Tucson. Maybe if I had been moved up more gradually to Double A for a while and eased into that, things might have been different. I have to admit I wasn't that patient either. I normally am, but I wasn't about that. I wanted to get back to the majors as fast as possible.

I do think that the Astros gave up on me too soon. On April 27, 1984, the Astros released me. They weren't giving me any more chances. My agent Tom Reich got a call from a team in Japan, but at that time it didn't feel right to me. I think I should have gone to Japan to try to play in 1984. I had the chance. I think it was the Tokyo Giants that were interested, but the team that wanted me sent a guy to Houston to try to sign me. I didn't feel great about it. It seemed as if it would have been too hard with the language barrier and me fighting to still get stronger. It's hard on all of the guys who go there.

They go to keep playing and to make money. One thing I know is that I wouldn't have blended in with being black and being so big. Given all of the upheaval I had been through in the last couple of years, it didn't feel right to dive into something like that. They tried to talk me into it, but I just said no.

One big reason was that the doctors in Houston wanted to keep monitoring my condition. I felt as if I would have been a guinea pig in Japan. The Japanese team was the only one that called. I didn't hear from any other major league teams asking me to try out for them. They all assumed I was finished. Everyone knew what had happened to my health, and everyone probably figured that if the Astros didn't think I could help them with my pitching, I couldn't help anyone else. I never got another phone call. Naturally those teams would be hesitant. I would've been hesitant, too.

While all of this was going on in my life, there was a strong depression factor. I was only 30 years old when the stroke got me. I was not thinking about a future career. I was thinking about the next batter I would face in the pennant race. There is always hindsight and shoulda, coulda, woulda. There was no good reason why my career should have been cut off then. God has his reasons, and I ultimately accepted that.

Looking back, I suppose I could have tried to hook on with another Triple A team just to show clubs what I had. If I did well, I could say, "Okay, I can pitch in Triple A. Now you can promote me." But after the Astros cut me loose and I turned down Japan, I didn't pursue baseball anymore.

That was the end of it for me when the Astros released me in 1984. My last game was pitched for the Daytona Beach Astros in rookie ball in 1983. It is hard to give up doing something that you love so much and you had done for so long. Even worse was that I wasn't going to something. I was being forced to leave something behind and I was already depressed about how my life was going. There is no doubt about it. Those were pretty tough times. Being turned out of baseball, though, was not the low point. Things were going to get worse.

16

Coping with Life After Baseball

Once J.R. Richard was felled by a stroke, newspapers around the country followed his progress every step of the way—from his release from Houston's Methodist Hospital, through his rehabilitation, to his promotion to the Astros roster in September of 1981, to his attempts to fight back to the majors through the minors.

However, there had been some alarming developments indicating that Richard was not his old self. During a practice session, a ball that was supposed to be a grounder turned into a line drive. The ball shot past Richard's head, but the scary thing was that he did not react by throwing up his glove for protection. He did not react at all. It was as if he did not see the liner coming. His depth perception was off. In a telling comment, Richard said, "It's like trying to find a ghost."

In March of 1982, when J.R. was at Astros spring training in Cocoa Beach, Florida, the *New York Post* wrote about his comeback efforts under the headline, "J.R's Last Stand." When veteran sportswriter Maury Allen reported that Richard was headed to the minors to try and piece his career back together, he said it might be J.R's last chance and he referred to Richard's case as "one of baseball's saddest stories." The report noted that Richard was overweight and that his arm was bothering him. His fastball was not being clocked at the speeds it once attained. The early returns and opinions on Richard's performance were not full of praise. General manager Al Rosen was contemplating having J.R. return to the minors well before the move was made. "We haven't even discussed this with him," Rosen said. "But it seems like the most logical thing for both J.R. and the club."

Richard grew up in a churchgoing environment, but when he was in the depths of his depression, he began thinking more about religion and his relationship with God. During that spring training, Richard told Houston newspaper baseball beat reporters that he had learned a lot and his beliefs were more ingrained and stronger. "I'm a better person now," Richard said. "I'm going to pitch in the big leagues this year, but I'm not sure I could get there without God. I've been reborn."

Although Richard's Triple A mound appearances were mostly disastrous in Tucson, once again near the end of that season, the Astros indicated they were going to bring him up and at the least he would pitch batting practice. But Richard never did regain his groove in Arizona.

When Richard gave his mound comeback still another shot in March of 1983, that progress was cut short by a left calf problem he incurred. Doctors examined him and discovered that their work on the transplant of an artery had backfired somewhat. Circulation to Richard's left leg was poor, and he required even more surgery.

Just about every time J.R. thought he was making the kind of progress showing he might reacquire his pitching magic, some part of his body failed him and set him back. The easiest thing for Richard to do was to give up, but he did not want to stop fighting. He always talked a good line. "I know I'll come back," he said politely but firmly many times. "But everybody doesn't believe like I do. When I do come back, when people see me pitch again, they'll be shocked off their feet."

The attempt was noble, but in the end ineffectual. The 1983 setback hurt the worst because the Astros seemed to like what they saw in J.R's arm in spring training. By then Bob Lillis was the manager and he told sportswriters that while it was unlikely Richard would open the season on the major league roster he did not rule out the big man again pitching for the club.

Richard trimmed down to his old pitching weight, tipping the scales at 240 pounds again. He spoke about how he became a good Christian. Then he was crushed when the Astros cut ties with him in 1984, and his reaction was to withdraw more into himself. J.R.'s effort and determination had won him new levels of respect from players he didn't even know, but when he signed off for good, brushed aside by the Astros and eschewing a chance to go to Japan, his closest friends were saddened.

While Richard professed to turning into a better man because of his troubles and a better Christian and he hid the depths of his emotions well, some former teammates believed he was more deeply affected than he let on. "I don't think J.R. stayed angry, but I think he was angry at one time," ex-Astros hurler Larry Dierker said.

Ralph Garr, the former Braves star from Richard's hometown of Ruston, was deeply disturbed by what transpired with Richard. He was dismayed that Richard had the stroke and saw his pitching career go up in smoke and upset that he had been portrayed as lazy. "When he had the stroke, that was the worst feeling in the world," Garr said. "It was like people thought he was jaking it. Why wouldn't you want to go out and pitch when you're the best in the world? I was disgusted with the whole thing. I think J.R. was very angry about all that happened to him, especially when he couldn't make a comeback. But I think he grew out of that. Sometimes you have to gather yourself up and make the best of it and move on."

Enos Cabell said he thought Richard always believed he could come back because of his background of success in every athletic endeavor he had ever tried. Why wouldn't that apply now? "It was tragic," Cabell said. "He was the man. He would probably have been in the Hall of Fame. He was my best friend. J.R. and I did everything together. I was from Compton, California, and we didn't fish. He even had me fishing. When he had the stroke, oh shoot, I cried a lot. When things first happened, J.R. was angry and bitter. I don't know how you could not be. He couldn't understand it. When you are at the top of the world, and it is all taken away from you. I think he was hurt about what went wrong."

J.R. Richard

When the Astros released me in early 1984, the first thing I did was grab my fishing rod and went fishing everywhere I could to try to enjoy myself away from baseball. I fished freshwater in Louisiana and I fished saltwater in Texas. I fished at home in Louisiana and I fished off of Galveston, Texas, in the bay. I caught red fish, flounder, speckled trout, grouper, and black drum. I didn't go out deep water fishing because I got sick from the waves if I did it.

I definitely had thoughts about how I could still be pitching. It took time to get past that. It took time to come to the point where I could accept that I was not pitching in the major leagues anymore. I was already depressed, and that did not help. When I say it took time, I mean it took a lot of time. I convinced myself that I had to laugh instead of cry, that I was a civilian. I wanted to live a good, fun life. That was my thinking, but you can't just snap your fingers and have it be so.

Maybe I was angry at the very beginning that the stroke had happened, but I wasn't angry at the Astros. I wasn't mad at the Astros. I was disappointed. God helped me come to terms with how things were. At some point you have to accept the fact that things happen and you have to go on with your life. You can't sit around and be mad at something for 20 years. You've got to go on with your life. I figured that God wanted me to do something different. It took me a long time to figure out what that was, but I did determine that God didn't want me to be a baseball pitcher anymore, and he did want me to be a preacher. That, though, did not come to me right away.

I felt cheated out of my baseball career. I was 30 years old and was pitching the best I had ever pitched. I don't know if I could have gotten better, but why not? I had been getting better each year. At the least I thought I would have been able to pitch for another six or seven years and maybe more. The way I was looking at it, I planned to pitch into my 40s. I was looking at a career of 20-plus years. Look at Nolan Ryan. He pitched for 27 years.

At that time I didn't think about how J.R. Richard would be remembered as a pitcher. My career was cut short, so my wins and strikeouts just stopped right there. I don't think it changes the memories for people who saw me pitch and who formed an opinion about how good I was. Other than that I didn't know how people's thoughts about me would change.

I tried not to let retirement from baseball change me, but it had to somewhat. For all of those years, I had been a baseball pitcher and now I wasn't. It wasn't as if I had planned ahead for retirement. This was all sudden. I was depressed about it. I didn't want to be where I was, but I was there. *So what do I do from here?* While I had brought myself back to a certain point of good conditioning from the stroke, there were other effects that hung around. It took me a while to regain my speech clearly. I got fatigued easily. The stroke affected me mentally. There were times I couldn't figure things out, so that became a hindrance. I had to do things in a certain order. I had to make lists or I would forget things. That was very frustrating at the time. Very frustrating.

Once the Astros let me go, I sort of cut ties with baseball for a while. I spent all my time fishing and stopped following the sport. I kind of took a break from it. Only once in a great while did I go to a game. There was a gap. To tell you the truth, there is still a gap. I still like the sport, but I don't follow it with the same intensity as I did then when I was involved. I took a big step backward from it starting in 1984. I had loved baseball and I wasn't part of it anymore. I didn't have anything to do with it. It wasn't my job. I wasn't pitching. I didn't belong to a team.

For a while I drifted a little bit. I couldn't think of what I wanted to do and I couldn't find something that I truly enjoyed doing like I had with baseball except fishing. I didn't want to stay at home all day doing nothing. I was still in a depression stage and I had to fight that. If I stayed home, I didn't have anything to do, and it was boring. I didn't really pursue much of anything. Fishing was my hobby, but it became my main outlet of how to spend my time. I was probably in a little bit of denial that baseball was over. I didn't want it to be over. I didn't want to believe that it was over.

Once the Astros released me, I didn't have anything to do with the team. I made a clean break from baseball. I didn't have any dealings with them. I didn't make any personal appearances. They didn't call me. The season was going on, and almost none of the ballplayers called. When you're playing everyone is gung ho, but once you aren't there anymore, you are not their friend. I tried to call some guys that I had faith in and tried to seek employment. When I was playing and in the limelight, there were always business people from the community around saying things like, "If you ever need a job, give me a call." It seemed that those people were always out to lunch when I called. They never came back from lunch, so that added a fresh layer to my depression.

I really was deeply depressed. If you feel that way, you can hardly function. You just sit around or lie around and don't do much of anything. You have no motivation. The hardest thing to do is to make yourself get out of the house and do something productive. I was plagued by the same question over and over: "Now what are you doing to do? What are you going to do next?" And I didn't have an answer.

Baseball fans have the idea that all players are rich. I made good money, but my divorce cost me a lot of money. I had to go to work. I wanted a new career. Nobody in baseball called with the offer of a coaching job or anything like that. I think it was because of the stroke. The stroke still had a hold on me physically and mentally. It affected my stamina and my memory. I remember one time I was selling cars and got interrupted by the phone. I wrote something down about a vehicle and went out to look for it. I lost track of what I was doing. My concentration was broken and I was a guy who had a great focus when I pitched.

For a while I sold mobile homes. I sold used cars and new cars. The businesses thought my name could be an advantage in Houston, that it would get people to come by. Well, people came by, but they didn't want to buy anything. They wanted to meet me and talk baseball. After a while I would say, "Aren't you interested in a mobile home?" They would say, "We've got to go somewhere. We'll be right back." You knew from the first words out of their mouths that they were lying. They just wanted to meet me and maybe get an autograph.

A sportswriter came to see me a year after the stroke when I was selling cars, and at that time, I still had some trouble with my thinking process and saying what I wanted to say. I said that if I tried to talk too fast I got messed up. I was still trying to have my mouth catch up with my brain. One thing that happened after I was paralyzed on my left side was that my mouth was twisted. The doctors told me to chew gum as much as I could. That exercised the muscles. It worked. My mouth isn't twisted anymore, but I still chew a lot of gum. I always have some with me. It's like lifting weights for my mouth.

When you have a stroke, your muscles become depleted of blood and lose their strength. That's why everything gets so twisted. I would say one of the main reasons I didn't stay all twisted up is that I was in great physical condition and I worked at the rehab. During this period I was still learning to recognize God and how to give him all the glory and honor. I realized that my life wasn't really my life. I was not in control of my life. I didn't control anything. As the Bible points out, you go through this life. So if you're going through, do you really control anything? You don't keep your heart beating. You don't know how to make your vision work. You don't keep your blood pressure regulated. You don't keep your heart regulated. What do you really control? What is really controlling you? In the Bible it talks about Joshua being at war and he prayed to God for him to have the sun sit still and blind his enemies. God made the sun sit still for Joshua to win that war. You want to talk about power; that's power.

I know that many people listening to me would be angry or bitter if something like that stroke happened to them and ended their chosen careers. Inner peace as I was getting to know God better helped me rise above that. I could be mad forever, but you have to get over it. You get over it and you go on.

In 1982 I sued the Astros' team doctor, Harold Brelsford, and doctors at Methodist Hospital in state district court. I charged them with medical malpractice and negligence for how I was dealt with after my tests that showed the blood clot and because they sent me back out to the street before I collapsed at the Dome. I settled out of court. We never went to trial. My attorney put the Astros and Methodist people together on one complaint, and that limited some of what we could do. I did get some money from that, but I had bought a new house with my second wife, and all of my money was going fast. I lost about $300,000 in an investment, too.

Sometime after my second divorce, when I was living in the house off of Interstate 45 in the Sageglen area, I gave up my home and moved into an apartment. It was just me. I wasn't married, and the kids were with my first wife. I was trying to start over with selling cars and mobile homes, but I had a very difficult time. Those were just jobs, not a new career. I was living the single life, but I was depressed. It always came back to that. I went to bed, got up from bed, cooked breakfast, ate, and got back into bed. That went on for a while.

I was out of baseball and I no longer had health insurance, so I couldn't afford to see a doctor and get medication for depression. By then I was 35 years old. That's too early to begin drawing a baseball pension. You don't qualify for that until you are 45. I didn't have any insurance. I had no salary coming in. I didn't have a car and had to take the bus everywhere.

I thought I had money saved from baseball, but after the divorce when I called my agent and attorney, they said, "What money?" I didn't take care of my money like I should have. I didn't throw it away, but the investments I had didn't work out. I bought a number of Arabian stallions, 10 or 12 of them, and they were kept in Arizona. When I went to check on them, I couldn't find them. I don't know whether someone left the gate open, whether they were out to pasture, or if they just got out. I have no clue. They disappeared. To this day I don't know what happened to them. The divorce cost me a lot of money.

It was only by God's grace that I was alive, but I was seriously depressed. That is being ill, too, but not everybody realizes that. Actually, at the time I didn't really understand what depression was. That was the kicker. I didn't even truly know that I was in a depression. I got some calls to make some autograph appearances. I was on my way to San Antonio, and my truck broke down. It blew a piston. I had to pull over and get a hotel room and spend a night. I left the truck at a gas station and had to rent another vehicle. I eventually had to have a new motor in my truck. But that cost a lot of money, and I couldn't pay the man. My truck got repossessed. I went outside and thought somebody had stolen my truck. I called the police, and they told me it had been repossessed.

Luckily, there was a Kroger store down the street so I didn't have to go far to buy groceries. I was not really eating well. I didn't have any knowledge about nutrition. I was eating a lot of soul food, but I was also eating a lot of stuff that was no good for me. I ate a lot of pork, ham hocks, all very salty. I ate and got full as a tick and then laid my sorry butt down next to the TV remote control. I'd just hang around and watch TV. I didn't have the will to make myself do more at that time.

Without insurance or finances, I didn't have the money to go to a doctor, but if I had realized that what I was feeling was a clinical depression, I would have tried to do something about it. I am sure that this was a backlash to me losing my baseball career, to the stroke leaving me less than fully healthy, to losing my money, to not being able to find a fulfilling job.

I could still put on a good face in public like when a sportswriter came to see me, though inside I was really down. I did ask the "Why me?" question often, but I wasn't bitter. Everyone asked me if I was. During a 1984 interview I said, "I call what happened to me the Big Trade. I traded baseball for the life of God." I said that and I meant that, but that didn't mean that life was always easy. I was only human, so I did go through a lot of thoughts and emotions. You get up to live or you lie down and die. I was trying to make the choice to get up and live. But I was just moping around. If you choose to do that, God isn't going to change it. He isn't going to change you. They don't move in heaven unless you move down here on earth first. You've got to pray. You've got to change first and then God will help you along to change things. You still have your will. Humans have free will, but God will guide you every day. Remember the phrase, "God helps those who help themselves."

As if the stroke was not bad enough, I also discovered that God was going to keep on testing me in ways I had not anticipated. I thought I had hit bottom when the stroke ruined my baseball career and took away my livelihood and I had been through two divorces. Soon enough I found out that my hard times were not over.

17

Life as a Homeless Vagabond

Demoralized, depressed, divorced, in mediocre health, and essentially on his own, J.R. Richard reached a dead-end of sorts. The jobs he worked for short stretches seemed like stop-gap gigs for only months at a time. Baseball was lost to him. He lost contact with people in his old orbits—from friends through his family, to wives, to baseball friends, who were busy with their own careers. He stopped reaching out to people. Although his increased faith in God gave him a layer of insulation against what seemed to be an increasingly cruel world, his loss of stamina, the confusion he sometimes faced, and his disregard of good health habits contributed to an iffy status.

Once a weight-room maven who liked to run and was proud of his 3 percent body fat, Richard didn't have the strength to lift weights with any regularity, nor did he have the stamina to jog for very long. His couch potato existence in front of the television set, combined with poor eating habits, caught up to him. The immediate years after the Astros released Richard were a very challenging time for the once physically dominant athlete who couldn't seem to muster the energy to reach out for help either.

With a bank account drained by his divorce settlement and lack of income coming in, Richard went into a downward spiral and lost the control of his life he had maintained. His vehicle repossessed, short on the rent, Richard became a quiet casualty of American society moving on without him able to maintain a foothold. Eventually, he lost his apartment as well and took refuge amongst the city of Houston's homeless. Years had passed since Richard lost his place in the limelight of Major League Baseball. Most of those who knew him had lost track of him, and his whatever-happened-to story turned out to be a shocking and upsetting one once it was revealed.

Richard became so strapped financially that he lost the house he and his second wife had purchased. He moved out with a feeling of desperation, put some of his belongings aside, and began moving from friend to friend, crashing on sofas, spending nights with them as long as he felt welcome. When he believed he had used up the goodwill he had accumulated with them, J.R. became homeless.

Over a period of a few months in late 1994 and early 1995, Richard lived under a bridge overpass at 59th and Beechnut Streets in Houston. Despite his formerly well-known face and persona, he went unrecognized. One of J.R.'s distinguishing characteristics was his size. A man who stands 6'8" and whose weight was climbing to the 300 mark does not blend in easily, but Richard did so. He was living out of context. No one made the connection that J.R. Richard, the famous pitcher, was the same person as this large African American man wearing somewhat tattered clothing. He stayed under the bridge for a week at a time over a three-month period, but sometimes he would drift back to a friend's house, relying on kindness to stay off the ground and under a roof.

In January of 1995, a Houston newspaper reporter discovered that J.R. Richard, one of the city's sports heroes, was living under this bridge only a few miles from the Astrodome where he had experienced some of his greatest glory and that he had just $20 in his pocket. The reaction was stunned disbelief by readers of *The Houston Post* and baseball fans, and sportswriters across the nation reacted similarly. The fans were shocked to hear that he had fallen so far. The reporters flocked to Richard to hear the story for themselves. It was an unfathomable predicament for a once prominent figure, one that had done marvelous things on the diamond and entertained millions with his brilliant skills, and both Houston residents and national baseball followers were dumbfounded by these revelations.

It didn't take a detective to point to the stroke as the root of all the problems that followed, and teammate and friend Enos Cabell unhappily watched Richard's life unravel. "It was a downward spiral from there," Cabell said. "It got worse and worse. He just had so many things go wrong. It was ironic that J.R. ran out of money. He had always been so generous helping people. He gave money away. If he had money with him and he saw someone in need on the street—like a homeless person—he would give him money. He thought he would be okay forever."

For someone like Ralph Garr, who had watched Richard grow up and star as the untouchable athlete in Ruston, Louisiana, and saw him make it to the top, it was particularly upsetting to learn of J.R.'s fall, first physically because of the stroke, and then economically after his already bad luck turned worse. "He was a sick man," Garr said. "Before that he could do anything. I don't know how much more down you can be."

Richard, though, was lifted up when he met Reverend Floyd Lewis, pastor of the Now Testament Church of Houston through Lewis' son, Bruce Williams, who was the manager of a Burger King. Lewis said that J.R. went into the hamburger establishment and asked for help. Williams told him Richard asked, "Can you feed me?"

At that point, Richard was not in touch with the Astros or other formerly important people in his life. "He was totally, totally invisible," Lewis said.

But through their association, Lewis said, Richard began working with the homeless and became known as an advocate for them, and J.R. reconnected with friends and the Astros. "I'm the one that got him back on his feet," Lewis said. "We brought him back to the surface."

J.R. Richard

After my stroke I couldn't jog for a period of time and I kept eating. I had been 240 pounds, and it was mostly muscle. From the way I ate and sitting around, I got up to 302 pounds. I had to change or that would kill me. Since I couldn't run, I started walking. I developed a ritual. I got up in the morning and sometimes I wouldn't even eat before going out the door. I'd walk four or five miles at a time, maybe even more sometimes. I just put on my walking outfit and left the house. I didn't have a time schedule. I would just walk. I didn't wear headphones and listen to music. I walked and looked around at the scenery. My goal was to get back into super shape.

What hindered me was how much time I had spent sitting around through the depression stage. I got really heavy and overweight. I was dieting and trying to lose it all back. I was still doing better than the doctors said I would. They had said early on that I wouldn't pitch again. They said I might not walk or talk again. They said I was lucky I didn't die.

My brain did not shut down, but there was a lack of oxygen, so I lost something. My memory wasn't as good. I did talk slowly for a while and I did have trouble coordinating my thoughts and my speech for a while. Some brain cells died, and, I guess, once they die they don't come back. My memory is pretty good most of the time, but it is sketchy some of the time. Some of the time period around my homelessness I have forgotten the details, but maybe that's something you don't want to remember as well as a game when you strike out 15 guys. I've never had trouble remembering beating the San Francisco Giants in my debut and striking out Willie Mays three times.

During the worst of my depression, when I wasn't working and I was wasting so much time, I had no money coming in, and one day it was all gone. I did feel lost for some of that time. I was relying on God, but I wasn't relying on too many people. They didn't really know my situation. My truck was repossessed. I didn't have money to pay the rent. I wasn't buying good food. Then I was homeless. I found a place to stay under a bridge like some other homeless people in Houston. Houston has a mild climate so you don't have to fear freezing to death in Houston if you are exposed to the elements.

Sometimes I would go to the home of a friend of mine named Patrick and eat there. Maybe I would stay over a night or two for a visit, get up in the morning, wash my clothes, and then go on my way back to 59th and Beechnut Streets. I knew I couldn't stay at his place all of the time, but he didn't give me any advice or tell me to call anyone for help because he didn't know my whole situation. He had a wife, and I felt like

I was intruding, so I didn't feel right staying there long. He didn't play any other role because I didn't tell him everything. I would just come to visit and stay over and then leave.

The bridge where I slept is not very far from the road. You always heard cars. People would drive by, the music blasting on their radios, or beeping their horns. A lot of people blew their horns. It could be noisy. There was a Houston pastor named Floyd Lewis who came to the bridge to talk to the homeless about God and to invite them to his Baptist church. It was called the Now Testament Church on Anderson Road in Houston. I had already begun a closer relationship to God, but I had so many setbacks that I was not sure exactly what I felt. I told people that I found God when I was homeless living under the bridge. That implies that God was lost, but he was never lost. I was lost. I wasn't even really looking for him. I was that lost.

When I was growing up in Louisiana, we attended a Baptist church. That was my exposure to religion, and everyone in the family went to church on Sunday besides my father. When I was playing baseball, I used to go to church on Sundays, too. I went regularly when the team was at home and I went sometimes on the road. Once, I went to church in New York City, and they took like seven collections during the service. You can't afford to be a member of that church. I thought they had to be killing people financially. It was just like, collection, collection, collection. I gave one time, and that was what I had.

During the time when I was homeless, I spent a lot of time reflecting and wondering how I could get out from under the bridge. This was in late 1994, early 1995. That was my first goal, to get out from under the bridge and get a place to live again. I prayed a lot and thought a lot about God during that time. I knew I had to get myself together. I felt I was a better person than I had been and that I should not be homeless. You don't live when you are homeless. Homelessness works its way inside you. You don't live in homelessness, you're part of homelessness.

That takes over your whole life. It gets to a point where you do not use the word homeless. It turns into survival. You aren't trying to hurt anybody, but you do what you have to do to survive. That's why some homeless people steal. Otherwise, they couldn't afford to eat. Some homeless people steal with the entire purpose of getting caught, arrested by the police, and sent to jail. That way for two or three days they have a roof over their heads and they get three meals a day. And they can stay warm. It's cold being on the streets. Even though Houston doesn't have winter weather like a Chicago or New York, if you are out there overnight and not well protected, you feel the cold.

So you take that chance. What else are they going to do with you? They lock you up. It's a good trade-off for a lot of people—a roof, warmth, food. My faith never wavered, but I still wondered how I got where I was. It seemed like life was moving so fast and I didn't know what was happening. I was walking around like a zombie. My memory of that time period isn't all that good. Some of it is a blur. At one point you just switch to survival time. You have to do that in order to sustain life.

There are some things you just don't recall. It seems that life was moving as fast as the cars passing by on the road or the bridge, and I was just standing in one place. And that was pretty much true. It was like that. I was depressed before I ever became homeless. Becoming homeless is very depressing to people. They get so depressed they don't want to go on. They don't want to live anymore. If you give up, you can't get any lower.

Sometimes, though, the only way God can get you to see what you need is to bring you to that low point. When you get there, you don't recognize anybody but God. God is the only one who can help you. It was proven to me that some men didn't care a hoot about me. Houston knew who I was. I played for the city's team. I was a member of the Astros. But there I was, homeless, on the street. God was the only one to turn to for me.

It is said that a smiling face is just a frown turned upside down. So everybody who smiles at you and pats you on the back is not necessarily your friend. One thing good about God is that eventually he lets you see who those people are. I'm speaking of that given time. Most people don't get tested as thoroughly as I did. When you have troubles, you learn things.

If you are well-off, famous, and playing a professional sport, you are very lucky. Unless you get into a situation like I did, you don't think it is either possible or logical. You would never think what happened to me—having a stroke, losing my money, becoming homeless—would happen unless you got into that position. You'd never think about such things if you were not in that position. If you are a millionaire, never in a million years do you think about becoming homeless. It would never cross your mind unless it was all taken away from you and you became homeless.

Life doesn't stop because you got knocked off a pedestal. No, it wasn't my fault that I had a stroke, and I did everything in my power to come back and pitch for the Astros, but I got released. I got divorced, and that's between two people. I lost my money and was taken advantage of in some cases. But I had to stop blaming other people for what happened to me. I had to look into myself and realize I could have done some things differently.

Yes, I was sick. I wasn't myself. Some things weren't really my fault. But I could have done things differently with my money, my savings. Maybe I could have made better investments. Things happen to you for a reason. Sometimes God loves you so much that he will allow these things to happen because he knows they will bring you closer to him. He was telling me how much he did love me. You can say that it is a mean way to show it, and it is.

But sometimes people are so bull-headed—like me— thinking you've got everything, thinking you've got to take on the world. You don't. I realized I wasn't in charge of anything. I was having trouble running my own life, never mind even thinking of running anyone else's life. I had to deal with my own life. The thought process started when I was living under that bridge. The comprehension that stemmed from that point didn't really dawn on me until I studied more. It was gradual. Then it became my focal point.

I reached the point of the reality of the moment where I had to put everything in order. Physically, I was older, in my thirties. I couldn't do the same things I used to do when I was younger. I realized the youngster was behind me then. But I also realized that my best years were in front of me because of the knowledge I had gained in my youth. I made mistakes and gained knowledge through my mistakes. If you make a mistake and don't learn anything, you repeat it. What is the benefit to you if you make a bad mistake and don't gain anything from it? Even though it wasn't my mistake to have a stroke, it had to be called a bad mistake in my life. It was something I couldn't do anything about.

I did not become homeless because I had a stroke, but everything that followed from it led to me being homeless. It wasn't my fault in general, and I don't think anybody would blame me for those things, but I couldn't sit around and be mad forever about yesterday.

Some people are living in the past. That's why they can't ever go forward. You have to let things go. A man who lives with a clenched fist can never get anything out of it and nothing can ever get in. Some people do the same old thing and expect a different result. If you don't change, how can you expect things to change around you? If you remain the same, things around you will also remain the same. Things change when you change.

One night when I was living under the bridge a guy named Chris Clark came by. He worked at the Westwood Golf Club, which is kind of an exclusive golfing club in Houston. I never understood if he was looking for me or he just found me by accident. I am a little fuzzy about the order of things from that time.

I know Floyd started bringing me to his church and I began preaching there. A newspaper reporter from *The Houston Post* came to me and wrote a story. I think Floyd put the attention on me. I can't remember. Maybe Chris had read the story and came looking for me. But he pulled up to the area by the bridge and started blowing the horn. Horns were always blowing around there so at first I ignored it. He blew the horn, and I didn't even acknowledge it. I didn't really care.

The cars passing overhead made a certain sound all of the time over and over again. You got to the point where you ignored it and went to sleep. You were so fatigued anyway. The homeless people told me that before I came there sometimes kids came by and shot into the crevices. I don't know if anyone got killed or not. It sounded like stupidity. There were a dozen or more people there each night. They were mostly guys, but there were some girls, and they were doing prostitution. The guys were also desperate. They panhandled all day and they might get $5. It was a desperation area. The police didn't disturb anybody.

I thought that as long as we were peaceful, the police wouldn't bother us. If you ran up to cars that stopped and demanded money, that might get reported, and the police would come by to see what was going on. Some of the homeless guys made the mistake of cursing people if they didn't give them money.

I was all scruffy and everything and I didn't really look like me. Chris didn't recognize me at first. He said, "That looks like J.R. Richard." He brought another guy around and came back to me. He picked me up at the bridge and took me out of there back to his house. I took the little old nothing that I had with me and I stayed with him at his house for quite a while. Some of my things had been put in storage, and we went and got those back.

There was a guy who lived near Chris named Doyle Jennings. I got cleaned up and started doing some work for the Able Asphalt Company that Doyle owned. Doyle had just paved the parking lot for a new apartment complex and he knew the owner. He helped me get an apartment in there.

I wouldn't have been able to afford to do that without Major League Baseball's emergency assistance fund for players who have fallen on hard times. It's called BAT for short. Joe

Black, who had been a very good pitcher for the Brooklyn Dodgers, later went to work for the commissioner's office counseling ex-players about career choices and then he became a member of the board of directors of BAT. He stepped in and got me help from BAT to pay my living expenses. Black played a huge role in turning my life around. I will be forever thankful to him and BAT.

I was living off the cuff. Thank God, there was Major League Baseball. I was only 35 and I couldn't qualify for a pension for 10 years. BAT saw to it that I got a new apartment and they took care of the rent. Joe hammered out all of the details. Joe worked it out so that everything was fine. I just paid the light bills and utilities. I was in good shape until I could draw my baseball pension.

18

Meeting Lula

J.R. Richard was 44 years old when he was discovered living under the Houston bridge, a location as temporary as could be. He told reporters that he had lost his last home two years earlier and had been living on the edge ever since as he continued to try to make his way and fought off depression and other side effects from the stroke that had ended his baseball career in 1980.

Some of the things that had led to his financial collapse included being fooled into making a $300,000 investment in a California oil deal that was not legitimate, the $700,000 divorce settlement with his first wife, being taken advantage of by his second wife, and having a start-up barbecue business fail. One of the first people in Richard's old orbit who caught wind of his predicament was former Astros star Jimmy Wynn. It wasn't as if Richard had a cell phone that he could be reached on, but Wynn reached out to Richard by attending a church feed for 100 homeless people that January and then attempted to resurrect his baseball connections by obtaining a job for him with the Astros.

It was Chris Clark from the country club and Floyd Lewis from the Baptist church who acted more swiftly to rescue Richard from his circumstances. The original story by *The Houston Post* was picked up by United Press International, the Associated Press, and *The New York Times*, among other news outlets. Richard did not seem at all surprised that other homeless people who stayed in the same highway underpass area did not recognize him. He said he told no one who he was. "I didn't want them to know who I was," Richard said. "I'm not happy being under a bridge, but now I know what those people go through. What I've tried to tell them and myself is that nothing lasts forever. Only death. There aren't too many people who knew exactly how bad off I've been." He said he was trusting God to help him "out of this mess."

Wynn made the effort on his own to check out reports of Richard's situation and said that as soon as he verified that J.R. had no home he wanted to do something about it "even if J.R. was too proud to do it himself. And J.R. is too proud."

Probably the first widespread images of homelessness transcending individual cases dates to the Great Depression that hit the United States in the late 1920s and early 1930s. Thousands upon thousands of Americans lost jobs, and homes and were uprooted. There seemed to be a fresh epidemic of homelessness in the world's richest country in the 1980s, and the problem, to some degree or another, has been on the nation's radar screen fairly steadily since.

Downtown Congregations Against Homelessness is a coalition of churches that continues to shine a spotlight on homelessness in the United States. As part of the group's values statement, it states that having a home is a human right. An article on the organization's website stated that homelessness in America has been documented since 1640, but at that time it was common to blame the victim. "In the 1640s," the article reads, "homelessness was seen as a moral deficiency, a character flaw. It was generally believed a good Christian, under God's grace, would naturally have their needs met."

According to a January 2012 report from the National Alliance to End Homelessness, on any given night in the United States nearly 634,000 people are without a home. Much like J.R. experienced, many people float from place to place when they do have a temporary opportunity to put a roof over their heads. There are more shelters, especially in large cities, that help take care of the homeless, but the individuals do not find permanent answers to their homeless situation. The shelters are stopovers. This organization estimates that 18 percent of those 630,000-plus people are "chronically homeless." They are the people who face the most serious problems. While a majority of those who are plagued by homelessness do find places in shelters, many others live on the streets or in automobiles, the report indicated. There has been an increase in the number of entire families who are homeless.

One conclusion of the report was that the federal government must build more units of affordable housing to help the homeless population. Years have passed since J.R. Richard was one of the homeless statistics in Houston, but the monitoring by such organizations with the agenda of eradicating the problem shows it is still a vexing and serious issue in the United States. After J.R was rescued from his situation and given a jump start by the Major League Assistance Program and friends, he gravitated toward working to help homeless individuals and to preach the word of God.

Although he initially worked with Lewis, Richard then became associate pastor at Mt. Pleasant Church in Houston. His sermons to the congregation reflected much of the thinking he focused on while living under the bridge and the conclusions he reached about God's love and God's influence. At one time *The 700 Club*, the nationally televised religious program that is the featured show on the Christian Broadcast Network, wrote a story about J.R. that was posted on its website.

In that story Richard said that baseball was part of his past life and that he has moved on to serving God. He said, "I'm not gonna say that I just woke up one morning and I'm all 'holier than thou.' No. God does things in time. I'm not perfect, but I'm working on perfection. The devil is not going to come to you in your strength. He's going to come to you in your weakness.

"You may give him a week, and when things don't work out, you say, 'Ah, forget about this God stuff.' But you've got to give him your life. If man would quit looking at himself and start looking to God, he'd become a lot better off."

Richard went from promoting the asphalt business to promoting God. He also invested considerable time in drawing attention to the plight of the homeless. After all, it was a problem that he was personally familiar with and he was sensitive to the issue. J.R. also married for a third time in 2010. He met his wife, Lula, through Mt. Hebron Church. Their first date, if it can be called that, consisted of riding the bus together. Richard was traveling by bus at that time and although he didn't really know Lula (they knew of each other following a quick introduction at a Christmas activity) he asked her to ride the bus back from a church event. She didn't want to, preferring to take a ride from a friend. But the friend was late, and she rode the bus with J.R. The only seat available was the seat next to J.R., so she had to sit with him.

After a service, when Lula was standing around in a group, the congregation's minister made chit-chat and said, "How did you all enjoy having a service with a celebrity?" Her reaction? "Everyone was looking around to see who the celebrity was?" Lula said. "So was I."

Lula was not really a baseball fan, but she had seen J.R. Richard play in the 1970s. "I knew who he was, but he looked different from then," she said. "I knew, but I wasn't interested. I just walked off. I wasn't at an Astros game. I was at work as manager of Houston Republic Bank, and they had the game on TV. We kept up with the important games at work."

She knew who J.R. Richard, the baseball player, was, but she did not know J.R. Richard. After the service she told her friend she would ride with her, but J.R. intercepted her and asked her to talk with him for a minute. On the bus he asked to borrow her Bible for a moment, and she said, "Why do you need my Bible? You've got your own." J.R. reiterated his request and said, "Well, you never know what God has in store for you." He wrote down his phone numbers in the Bible. "You never know," he said. "You may need to talk to me or you may need me for something."

They talked on the bus ride and then when the bus parked at their church they stayed on the bus and talked some more. When they disembarked Lula went to her car, and J.R. went to his truck, each going their separate ways. "Actually, he was really impressive," Lula said. "Lord have mercy. I never say that about anyone. Any time I have, I have ended up being married to him. The only two people I ever said that about I did marry. The Bible says that life and death are in the power of your tongue. You have to be careful what you say because it will come right back on you."

The next day, Monday, Lula kept hearing a voice in her head saying, *Call him.* She talked back to herself saying, *I'm not calling him.* "I heard this voice pushing me to call, and I kept saying, 'Uh, uh,'" Lula said. "Tuesday, it was the same thing. I said, 'Uh, uh, I'm not calling.' On the Wednesday I finally gave in and called him. He said,

'Oh, that's confirmation.' I said, 'Why confirmation? Have you been praying on me?' He said, 'Yes.' I about fell down because God had been pushing me to call when I didn't want to call."

For Lula this was a somewhat awkward situation. She was resisting J.R. but felt she was being directed toward something. "I knew that God was showing him to me," Lula said. "When J.R. joined our church and he walked up to the pulpit, there was a halo over him. It was a bright light. All I could see was light. He was lit up from the floor, and there was a light all the way around him. I looked at that and I turned my head away. I looked back again, and there was the same thing. I said, 'Lord, I don't know what you are doing, but I'm not interested.' God shows you things. It's up to you to follow them. That was in a November. We had that time on the bus in March, March 7. I knew that God was trying to do something, but I didn't know what it was. We got married two years later."

J.R. Richard

I had never forsaken religion, but my relationship with God changed after I was homeless. I became more dedicated. I became more consistent. And through the Now Testament Church, I began working directly with homeless people to help them. Floyd Lewis already had a program in place, and I joined up through the church. I started cooking for the homeless—I always liked cooking—and we served meals on Sundays. We went out and picked up homeless people in a van and brought them to the church to feed them.

After being homeless myself, it was easy for me to relate to the problems of the homeless. Having a roof over your head was critically important, but other problems came hand-in-hand with being homeless since homelessness was a byproduct of having no money. By that I mean, that homeless people are often hungry, too.

We tried to lend a hand, to talk to these people. You have to realize that usually it isn't a quick fix. Usually people get to the point of being homeless gradually over a period of time. It's going to take time to fix things, too. Being homeless you go into survival mode, and that's sometimes just existing one day at a time and from one meal at a time. Homelessness takes over your whole life. You get into a kind of rut. You drift along. You have no responsibilities.

The average person who has a home and commutes to work and drives by people living on the street doesn't really understand the homeless. I don't know how much they think about it, but they don't realize how it happens to people. The only way they can understand it is if they are homeless. They have to get out of their fancy houses, put up their car keys, take off their normal clothes, and spend a couple of nights on the streets. Anyone who did that would have respect for his own life, would cherish his life a lot more, and look at homelessness in a whole new way.

Of course a truly homeless person can't just walk away and go back to a better life. But someone who put themselves in a homeless person's shoes would change their outlook. First, they would learn that, even though people are homeless, they are still people and they deserve respect. They should be treated as people. Even if you give them food or money, give them a dollar, treat them as people. Until you are there, you don't know what a dollar can mean, but you don't know what it can mean if you are treated poorly when you get that dollar. In a sense you can't blame those people. Homeless people are in survival mode, and you are not. You are in a different situation. You have money, a house, a car, a job. If something happens to you in that circumstance, you are going to fight it. You aren't going to sit around and wait for things to get worse. If you are homeless, you are probably beaten down by all of the things that have happened to you to get there. You may not have the spirit left to fight back. You sit around. You are only trying to survive.

So often you hear the phrase that we live in the richest country in the world, but if you are homeless, that doesn't make any difference. You are not part of the richest country in the world. If the United States has all of these resources and has all of this money, then it should be better equipped to deal with the problem of homelessness. The government doesn't seem prepared to solve this problem. They could be doing more. We spend billions and billions of dollars on wars overseas. They could take some of that money and spend it on Americans at home who are homeless. For one thing the agencies that study homelessness all say that thousands and thousands of the homeless are veterans. So we send Americans off to fight wars overseas, and they come back and they become homeless? That doesn't sound fair. The government isn't doing enough. It seems to be that the people who work on trying to help the homeless are churches and charities. There needs to be more for homeless and people and for those veterans who come home and are in trouble. You've got thousands of veterans who go overseas to Iraq, Iran, wherever in the Middle East and they come back and then what? It's insane. It's crazy. They deal with problems we don't even understand like Agent Orange.

I worked with Floyd Lewis helping the homeless for six or seven years. It's hard. You want to help people, but it's not easy to get through to them so they can help themselves. The saying goes, "that if you give a man a fish he can eat for a day, but if you teach him how to fish he can eat for a lifetime." Homeless people are in the desperate mode that means going from one meal to the next. Sometimes it's tough to penetrate that kind of thinking and push them to do more. The truth is that the way to fix things is not to sit on your butt and wait on somebody to come help you. You have to get up and do something with your life. That's the truth and not everybody wants to hear the truth.

I know because I was there. There was a stage that I passed through when I was depressed when I did not want to do anything but lie around. Some of them are—I won't say content—but are willing to lie around. Not everybody is going to respond to the message—no matter what is in your heart and no matter how much you want to help them.

After spending years working with Floyd at Now Testament Church, I moved over to Mt. Pleasant church where I became associate pastor. Then I switched to Mt. Hebron. I met my current wife, Lula, through that church. A lot of people in our lives think we have been together forever, but we didn't meet until 2000. She was attending one church and switched over to my church. All of the churches are in Houston just in different parts of town.

We were introduced at a Christmas event at the church by a friend named Betty Grove. It wasn't an introduction to fix us up but just a polite thing, a casual introduction. After that I kept trying, but I wasn't getting anywhere, not then. The funny thing about the bus ride when we sat together was that Lula had been fasting, and now it was over so she was eating and eating. Later, she said she thought she made a bad impression on me. I was just watching her eat and I said, "Are you hungry or something?" She hadn't had anything to eat since the night before. The reason she was fasting, she said, was for peace of mind. Her husband had died not long before.

Our real first date was going out to eat. We went to a Ruth's Chris Steak House. We courted for a couple of years and we got married five years ago. I'm happier than I've ever been since I married my soul mate.

19

Playing in the Senior League

Once the Astros released J.R. in April of 1984, and he declined an offer to resume his career in Japan, it seemed certain that Richard would never again pitch top-level baseball. If he ever threw off a mound again, it would be for an honorary first-pitch or just fooling around. Following Richard's other challenges from divorce, to financial losses, to losing his home, he drifted away from baseball completely. For years he barely followed the sport that he had enjoyed. So it was surprising when J.R. Richard's name surfaced with the fledgling Senior Professional Baseball Association in 1989.

This brainstorm was intended to give older former major league-caliber players a second shot at their youth. Just like the seniors golf tour that enabled plus-50 Professional Golf Association competitors to continue playing, this new baseball game promised to provide an outlet for players 35-and-up (except for catchers, whose wear and tear allowed them to come aboard at 32).

The league built its entire operation in Florida. The idea was to attract the millions of tourists who escaped cold weather for vacations and to appeal to the senior citizen population whose baseball fans would remember the older guys. Instead of a single old-timers game that might be organized by one team this was an old-timers league.

Some big names were attracted and participated in the league that lasted most of two seasons and into 1991. Among the slew of well-known players who gave it a try were Ferguson Jenkins, Rollie Fingers, Vida Blue, Jon Matlack, Dock Ellis, Steve Kemp, Ron LeFlore, Al Oliver, Manny Sanguillen, Bert Campaneris, Luis Tiant, Dave Kingman, knuckleballer Dan Boone, who parlayed his involvement into a major league job, and Richard's old teammate Joaquin Andujar.

Eight teams competed in the first season using such names as the St. Petersburg Pelicans, the Orlando Juice, and the West Palm Beach Tropics. However familiar with the game they were, Floridians proved to be more interested in televised football and basketball and such pleasures as swimming, fishing, and boating than they were intrigued by seniors baseball. They confined their continuing allegiance to baseball in spring training. The noble experiment league failed within a season-and-a-half.

Richard was 39 in 1989. He had been out of baseball for several years, but when his name popped up as an eligible player, he was pleased to get the opportunity to throw again. Hadn't he made it back to pitching 90 mph after the stroke? He was interested to see what he could do but was probably more optimistic than others.

It was exciting for him to get back into the game after a long absence. While neither the league nor J.R.'s baseball return lasted very long, it served as a gateway for him to reconnect with fellow players of his generation in the sport and spurred him to begin making public autograph appearances, events that tied in with the Astros, and to make out-of-town trips for charitable causes.

Once he and his wife were together, Lula began joining J.R. for the events. She had never been much of a baseball fan and in only the most general of ways a follower of the Houston Astros. All that she knew about J.R.'s past were the stories he told her. When the opportunities for J.R. to make the rounds of ballplayer-related events arose, she began traveling with him. In that manner the baseball world opened up for her, and she got to meet and know some of Richards' old teammates and the ex-players whom he once struck out. "I go to all of them," Lula Richard said. "I'm a participant in all of them now. I go to different functions, autograph signings, and celebrity golf tournaments. We've gone to New York quite a bit. We got to go to California. We went to Oklahoma, Phoenix, Arizona, and Alaska. We like to go to the Joe Niekro Foundation fund-raisers. Joe was one of J.R's teammates and he passed away from a brain aneurysm. They raise money for research to prevent aneurysms and strokes. We go to many Astros events at Minute Maid Park. Many times J.R. has said of some individual, 'We used to play together' or 'We were teammates together.' These events help me put a face to the name.

"J.R. is friendly with Dusty Baker, and he was one of those people that was only a name to me, and then I met him, and he became a person. To be honest J.R. is better known than I anticipated. We go to autograph signings, and there are hundreds of people from everywhere. They know him, his record, and his statistics. When we got together, I thought baseball was over for him. I found out it's not. It has been fun. I have really met a lot of nice people. Some of them I am not even sure if he played with the guys or not. Jimmy Wynn? He and his wife have become really close. I met her because we were in the same Christian loop. We became really good friends. Sometimes we were both at the same Astros event and we would just talk and talk, not about baseball. We talked about God. It's very good when you can find people that love the Lord as much as you do. Good friends in any walk of life are hard to come by and good to have. I really cherish her friendship."

That is the closest of friendships Lula Richard has formed as an offshoot of J.R.'s baseball. "I have met a lot of the other ladies, but a lot of them talk amongst themselves, and some of them talk religion, but they are not really on the same path as I am," she said. "When you find someone else whose heart is truly with God, you hold onto that, and cherish that."

J.R. even made new friends stemming from baseball a second time around. Although they did overlap in the big leagues, Richard and Jenkins didn't see much of one another during their playing days. "I have gotten to know him a lot better since we retired," said Jenkins, who stages an annual fund-raising golf tournament in Canada and has regularly invited Richard.

Both Jenkins and Richard enjoy golf and are passionate about fishing. Usually the celebrities who help out Jenkins are rewarded with a day of fishing before the tournament begins.

"He's a bit of a golfer and he likes to fish the way I do," Jenkins said. "J.R. was on the verge of becoming a great star and seemed to be on his way to putting up Hall of Fame numbers. He could have put a string of 20-win seasons together. He was young. When he comes to the tournament, he never talks about the stroke or the things that happened to him. He's never really brought it up. I think he's really tuned it out."

J.R. Richard

One day I received a phone call from some people involved with the Orlando Juice of the Senior Professional Baseball Association. The call came in 1989, nine years after I had last played for the Astros. I was excited when I heard they were going to be starting this league and that I might have an opportunity to play. It got me going about baseball again. I thought, *Go on back and get your old groove back.* That's what it felt like. A number of years passed, but it rekindled my love of baseball. Baseball is something that really gets into your blood and it had gotten into my blood at a young age.

Over the years with hard work, I had sacrificed a lot to play baseball. Baseball was my life, and I gave my all to be the best I could be in the game. Nothing else really mattered when I was fighting to be the best. I was married, but baseball was still the No. 1 thing. Part of my thinking was that the doctors had said I would never pitch, walk, or talk again, and I had proven everybody wrong up until then. I didn't care what the doctors said. I knew what I was going to do. Sure, there's a part of you that believes what they say. But I believed what I said. The doctors' predictions had been so negative. At the least I knew they weren't going to stop me from trying. They weren't baseball experts. I wasn't even sure they were medical experts the way I was treated.

Jose Cruz was my teammate again. Jack Billingham was pitching there. You know who was catching? Bruce Bochy, the manager who has just won his third World Series title with the San Francisco Giants.

For me to go to Orlando and play was very satisfying, gratifying, and fun. I still threw pretty hard. My location wasn't the greatest. My control wasn't the best. I didn't realize I had to learn to pitch all over again. I had to redo things. I wanted to make the most of it. After all of that time away, though, I wasn't in top shape and I wasn't nearly as good as I had been.

There was a problem with money on that team, too. My friend, Jose, almost won the batting championship and didn't get paid. I don't think he ever got his money. I did fairly well, but I could have done better if given some time. It was just one of those things. I had the same competitive attitude to throw the ball past people and I did throw it by quite a few, but I didn't have the control. It didn't last long. Neither did the league for that matter. They never made any money because the attendance wasn't very good.

I heard even the concessions weren't making money. That's about as hard to do as a casino going bankrupt. When I was down in Orlando staying in a hotel, someone broke in and stole all of my jewelry. That was a blow, but they were just material objects, and I didn't make a big deal about it. One of the consequences of the stroke was that I became very passive. When the jewelry was stolen, I said, "God is going to give it back to me." I believed that and went on.

Trying out for the Orlando Juice and the Senior League was fun while it lasted, but that was the end of me and pitching. It was a last try. After that, however, I was in touch with more guys in baseball. I was out there more visibly than I had been. I don't know what people thought about me after hearing about the stroke and being homeless and weighing 300 pounds. But I lost weight—I am never going to be a little guy—and even though I have never been as strong as I was before the stroke, most of the lasting effects on me are not visible to the average person.

My mouth straightened out. My left arm and leg got stronger. I look fine. People can't tell that I had a stroke just by looking at me. Some baseball fans remember that I was homeless and some don't, especially if they are younger. When

I go to a sports autograph show, I meet a lot of fans who are fun to talk to. The older ones saw me play and strike out a lot of guys. They remember those seasons when I struck out 300 batters.

Younger fans may have read up on me if they are coming to the show. Everyone is impressed by those 300 strikeouts. If you are a younger baseball fan, you never saw anyone do it and you might never see anyone do it again. A young fan might come with his dad or his uncle or cousin or something. Once in a while I overhear comments from those waiting and an adult will say, "That's J.R. Richard. He was one of the fastest pitchers of all time." That makes you feel good.

I began to enjoy going to memorabilia shows and making appearances through the Astros. I still get mail asking for my autograph. What I don't like is people who sell them on the Internet. Some people ask for several autographs, and they don't want them personalized. When that happens, you kind of know they are going to sell them.

If someone asks me to write "For Bob" on a card or a photograph, I know they really are a fan and they want to save that souvenir for themselves. People have told me, and I have seen it on the computer sometimes, that there are things for sale that I signed. I signed them as a favor, and people are putting them out there to sell.

I try to keep a low profile away from events. I don't want people writing to me and sending me stuff to sign at home. I would say I get about 10 letters a month, but I am sure it would be more if they could find me. They just don't know where I am. I have a website set up for that. We get a lot of cards, baseballs, and pictures for me to sign. We just got it up last summer. A friend of mine, Jimmy Valentine, runs it for me. It can be a lot of work.

When I get interviewed, I get asked a lot of questions about my playing days. People always ask me who was the toughest batter for me to face, but I don't remember anyone being that consistent against me. I didn't worry about who was coming up to hit or who I was pitching against. If there was another team's ace coming up in the rotation, I didn't pick and choose. I would be happy to pitch against them. I was like a bulldog. If it was a good pitcher, I didn't mind pitching against them. If it was a good hitter, it didn't matter. If you stepped into the batter's box, it was you against me. I didn't focus on one guy or another. There wasn't anybody who was special. They all put their pants on one leg at a time. I loved the challenge. I felt like I was the king of the hill, and they had to beat me. I was the boss.

There were a lot of good players that I admired. I admired Joe Morgan. I admired Pete Rose and Ozzie Smith for their talent. Some of my teammates I admired like Enos Cabell and Bob Watson. Astros shortstop Craig Reynolds made some All-Star teams. I admired his ability in the field.

Alan Ashby handled the ball so well as a catcher. A pitcher's relationship with his catcher is priceless. It helps to have your minds on the same wavelength. It's very important that he thinks the way you do. It can get tedious if you're not thinking alike, and you're standing out there on the mound shaking off this sign and shaking off that sign. It makes it harder when the hitter is trying to zero in on you. If you agree right away, the hitter doesn't have as much time to think about what you're doing. You want to keep him off balance and work quickly like snapping your fingers fast. You don't want to give him time to get comfortable. You want the time from when you release the ball to when he can pick it up and swing to go by like that.

When I was young, my favorite pitcher was Bob Gibson because of the way he pitched in the World Series. He was always big when it counted. I really liked him. I tried to develop his attitude. He didn't want to make friends with players on other teams. His attitude was like he was mad at you all of the time. He looked at you as if you were trying to steal food off of his plate. When you came to bat, if he was winding up, you didn't dare step out. If you did, the next one was right in there at your head.

He had the reputation that he wouldn't talk to other players, but I got to know him after he got out of baseball. It was through a function that The Black Aces held. Another pitcher who was very good that I didn't know very well was Tom Seaver. I did hit a home run off of him. I admired some of my Houston teammates like Don Wilson and Larry Dierker. Steve Carlton was a stud.

Unfortunately, there is still racism in the game. They don't seem to be recruiting black guys to play anymore. The numbers keep shrinking. I know a lot of young African Americans have turned to basketball and football, but some of that is because they don't have the same opportunities to play baseball when they are young. Baseball needs to work very hard at that. I don't think baseball is giving young black kids enough incentive to play baseball. One reason is that there aren't good fields in a lot of neighborhoods where black kids live. A young pitcher goes out there and he wants to throw and the grass is up to his knees. They don't have manicured fields.

So many fields have gone away in big cities where the talent is. Those same kids can always find a basketball court. I know that baseball got Hall of Famer Frank Robinson involved in Major League Baseball youth academies. That's a start. I guess they're trying. That's important. In Houston they've got kids in the Fifth Ward who want to play baseball, but they don't have the finances or transportation to get to other parts of the city to play on a good field.

There need to be more fields spread around in big cities so every kid can play on a good diamond. The fields don't have to be immaculate. You can fix up some existing places. You can start church leagues. You get a good speaker to come in and talk to the kids and get some responsible adults as managers and coaches and form a league.

In the old days, kids just went out and played on their own. These days parents are worried about crime and their kids getting into trouble, so activities have to be organized with supervision. There is too much crime and danger. There are also so many more things kids can get involved in without playing baseball. They'd rather sit at home with their bedroom door locked playing games. They put on ear phones, play videos, and listen to music all at the same time. I don't know how they can do that all at once.

Maybe more kids should learn how to throw the knuckleball. There are hardly any of those guys. Joe Niekro, he was a guy that was in a class by himself the way he threw it. If you have a good knuckleball, you can be effective. Joe could make the ball dance all over the place. Although there were times I watched a knuckleball guy struggle with his control. Oh man, if the wind was blowing, that made it hard. They just throw it up there. They don't know what the ball's going to do from one minute to the next. But a lot of those knuckleball pitchers have the longest careers of all. Sometimes those knuckleball pitchers last five or six years beyond other pitchers because they can still throw that floater and not hurt their arm. I never threw one. I tried a couple but not with the grip most of those guys use. It didn't work for me. Not even with a football. I couldn't get the ball to drop. I used what God gave me, and that was my fastball.

I would like to teach the game. Just a little bit. There are times that the Astros get requests for me specifically to make an appearance and they pass it on to me. It might be a little league thing, a banquet, or for a Triple A team. They are a clearinghouse for those types of things. Someone calls the Astros and says they would like to have J.R. Richard appear at their function, and they touch base with me. My connection to the Astros does come up, and it always will. I never had another major league team and I still live in Houston.

For a time when things weren't going very well in my life, I forgot all about baseball and how much I loved it. I just put it out of my mind and considered it to be gone and in my past. But now that I make appearances through the Astros and sign autographs at shows, I do think more about baseball again.

20

Reconciling with the National Pastime

As evidence that J.R. Richard was back in the fold with the Houston Astros, his presence was highlighted during the season-long team 50th anniversary celebrations in 2012. Founded as the Houston Colt .45s in 1962, the franchise scheduled a series of what it termed "Flashback Fridays" throughout the 2012 campaign.

On June 1 J.R. was the featured player and he was inducted into the team's Walk of Fame. Outside Minute Maid Park on Texas Avenue, there is a walkway akin to the Hollywood Walk of Fame with its terrazzo sidewalks and gold stars inlaid into the California turf. As part of the day's celebration, the Astros wore their old 1970s rainbow-splashed uniform tops. "I'm going to enjoy [the Walk of Fame event]," he said. "I think anything I can do to put a smile on someone's face does my heart good."

Richard's induction into the Walk of Fame took place in late afternoon before a night home game, and in-between the honors recognition and the first pitch, he signed autographs. It was Richard who was selected to throw that first pitch, though at a speed considerably slower than he attained in his prime. "It's just going to be nice and easy. I ain't going to hurt nobody," he joked. During an interview leading up to his star being unveiled, Richard wore a hat displaying the message, "GOD IS GOOD ALL THE TIME."

The occasion, 32 years removed from the 1980 pennant race and J.R.'s stroke, provided some nice memories. Art Howe, who was a Richard teammate and later managed the Astros, said that if Richard had remained healthy that season he was sure Houston would have won the World Series. He also believed Richard was in his prime and still improving when illness ended his career. "He kept getting better than the year before, if it was possible," Howe said. "This guy was on another planet."

Richard and his wife Lula regularly attend Astros home games, making it to several games per homestand. Given his stature, J.R. is able to procure preferred parking close to a non-public entrance, and it is a handicapped space. That is because one of the long-term effects of his stroke, coupled with the aging process—he is now in his 60s—means that J.R. cannot walk long distances without feeling fatigued. On one particular game day in August of 2014, however, Richard walked part-way around the ballpark to visit his star on the sidewalk. Not many fans, who were hurrying to their seats in time for the game, recognized him or were too busy to hail him. However, some yelled his name. A couple of Astros fans, acting as if they had known him his whole life, stopped to chat. The open and friendly J.R. treated them all as if they were old friends, only afterward mentioning that he had never met those people before.

For Lula and J.R., the trips to the ballpark seem as enjoyable for the social component as for the baseball. Walking in the door, walking along concourses, stopping in the press box, taking seats on the left-field side, the Richards met with and chatted with numerous team employees. Ticket takers and ushers seemed pleased to just say hello. The security guard at the gate smiled. "My name is Richard, too," he said. "We may be kin." Richard smiled back and said, "We may be." That night former Richard teammates and pals Jose Cruz and Enos Cabell were also in the house. Hugs were shared. "He's the best fisherman I ever saw," Cruz said of Richard.

The Astros were heading to another poor finish—they ended up 70–92—and attendance was light on a weekday evening. In fact the announced attendance of 17,345 seemed wildly exaggerated. Marveling at the paucity of the crowd in the domed, air-conditioned venue, it was noted to J.R., "You may personally know everyone here tonight." He went along. "You're right. I just can't remember their names."

Richard watched the Astros play with a critical eye (and a more involved one lately), and given the state of the Astros, there was a lot to criticize. He saw potential in some of the young players and commented, "They are improving." He liked Jon Singleton's swing and believed that Dexter Fowler could hit 50 home runs. Only compliments poured forth about Jose Altuve, who was on his way to winning the American League batting title.

At one point J.R. was approached by two huge fans. The guys both wore Astros jerseys and sombreros. One had the biggest mustache you'll ever see. It probably could be spotted from a quarter of a mile away without a telescope. He looked at J.R. and said, "We need you." J.R. said, "Call me in the eighth inning." A short while later Mr. Mustache, who said he had previously seen Richard at an Astros event, returned and requested an autograph. And then a different fan approached his seat, and Richard signed a glove.

Displayed were retired numbers worn by Jeff Bagwell, Craig Biggio, Larry Dierker, Jim Umbricht, Jim Wynn, Jose Cruz, Mike Scott,

Don Wilson, Nolan Ryan, and the 42 worn by Jackie Robinson that is retired by all teams. Richard did say that he hopes one day the Astros will retire his No. 50 jersey, something that has not occurred yet. With a backdrop of his achievements, it is not difficult to understand why Richard feels he belongs among them.

As Richard graciously interacted with a small number of fans and closely eyed play on the Minute Maid field, Lula Richard ate a dinner consisting of a large plate of nachos. She has become a baseball fan by association. Other sports engaged her growing up and as a younger woman. She played basketball, volleyball, and ran track. She did play softball, but she didn't love baseball. "Baseball has always been slow for me," Lula said. "I enjoyed playing softball, and it was easier for me to play than watch. I never really went to baseball games for that reason. It would have been fun and exciting to watch J.R. pitch because he is my husband. God knows best. It was not meant for me to be there. You don't want to be with someone because of what they do but because of who they are. You want to be with them because it is true love. I'm grateful for that. Fame would have been fine but so be it. There still is some, and it surprises me all of the autographs J.R. is asked to sign."

J.R. Richard

Probably the event that really put me back on the map with baseball and with Astros fans was the Fanfest at the 2004 All-Star Game. The game was played at Minute Maid Park, and in the days leading up to it, Major League Baseball schedules all kinds of events.

A lot of former players came and made appearances, and I was part of the autograph signing. I signed about 6,000 autographs in a couple of days. I don't think the line ever stopped. They just had to cut it off. Some people stood in line, came through, went to the back of the line, and came through again. There were people up the ying-yang. I was saying, "Where in the world are all of these people coming from?"

I never had an arm injury, but I could have gone on the disabled list after that just from signing my name. There were so many people. There were also girls out there who wanted autographs, and they would leave you their phone number. They were trying to hit on you. I was married and I wasn't interested. I didn't want to meet them.

Almost all of the people are very nice. They are glad to meet you. But there is always one a-hole. At a different autograph signing, one guy came in who had read about me and he wanted to debate the Bible with me. He is telling me this and that, and I said, "I understand all of that. Your point is?" He held out his hand for an autograph, to sign his hand. Then he wouldn't pay the $5 it cost. He said, "I ain't paying no man $5 for an autograph." I should have known he was going to be hostile. I should have said for him to pay the $5 first and then I would sign his hand. If not, "Thank you very much and I'll talk to you later." But I wasn't going to sit there and debate the Bible with him in the middle of an autograph session. There are all kinds of people out there.

After they retire most ballplayers will say they miss the clubhouse. Being around your teammates and other players is probably one of the best things about being in the game. Most of the guys were great over the years. You could never get along with all 25 guys, and there were always some that seemed to have some resentment in them and toward you. They may not have said anything—and I may be wrong—but you are crazy if you think that some people just are going to be your friends even if you are teammates. You can hear it in their voices or their conversation. You have a sixth sense that reveals it to you.

You also make associations that last forever. I differentiate between associates and friends. Because of what I've seen and learned, I have to say that you don't have many friends. You have a lot more associates. There is camaraderie between individuals as players. You are always a member of that group. You played. Some are nice guys, and some are not. But you are identified with baseball. Athletes love to be around other athletes because of the shared experiences. That's why those golf tournaments with ex-athletes are great for charities and why guys enjoy playing in them. Athletes connect with each other. That's a good thing. It is even more enjoyable connecting with athletes who played other sports like football, basketball, and hockey, and you compare notes about experiences. That's like my friend Fred Dean from Ruston who made it into the Pro Football Hall of Fame. When I first knew him, I didn't have a clue that he was going to make it. He grew up to become very big and he was very good at what he did. He represents another claim to fame for Ruston, Louisiana.

After a gap of some years, I am back to watching baseball much more often again. I go to the games with my wife. I watch some on TV. I know who the players are. I have ended up doing more public relations work and autograph signings now than when I was in baseball. I get quite a bit of fan mail.

I definitely think one reason why fans remember me are the strikeouts. They know that they aren't going to see a pitcher with 300 strikeouts anymore, and strikeouts are a part of the game that gives them a charge. Fans respond more to a strikeout than a ground-out. They count the same as one out, but scouts get excited by strikeouts, too. That's one thing that helped me. If you get a lot of strikeouts, it means the opponents aren't even putting the bat on the ball. It makes you look more dominating. I think the strikeouts helped catapult me into the major leagues, especially after playing winter ball in the Dominican Republic. I enjoyed performing and I got a lot of pleasure out of striking out hitters.

Pitching is so much different in the modern game. You have all of these specialists who only pitch one-third of an inning or one inning. They start every five days and never even think they are going to throw a complete game. The minimum salary is a $500,000, and they don't mind sitting around for it. They are satisfied with all of that. How can they sit around and just say, "I made it." They should realize it could be all over tomorrow. That's what happened to me.

These pitch counts are absurd. Pitchers don't even practice to be out there for nine innings. They pitch five or six innings and they are through. Six innings is a quality start. If you throw seven innings, you are a master. Today's games take so long, too, maybe because they're always changing pitchers. I pitched complete games that took less than two hours. I had a certain rhythm. As soon as I got the ball back from the catcher, it would go. I didn't waste time. They are talking about passing a rule that says a pitcher must throw the ball within 30 seconds. I probably threw it quicker than that. I would be against the rule, though, because every pitcher is different. You would have to put a rule in at the same time, saying the batter couldn't keep stepping out. That's the thing that slows some pitchers down, a batter digging a hole in the batter's box, holding his hand up, and then stepping out.

Most of my souvenirs from baseball are in my head, and my memory is not perfect from the stroke. I have some baseballs from games that I won, though I don't keep them out on display at home. I have a uniform jersey. I gave a lot of things away, but what I have now I am going to keep. If I knew then what I know now, I would have taken one of everything, shoes, socks, underwear, shirts, the whole nine yards, had them cleaned, and put in a special container. Then I would have stuck them in my closet. Right now I don't even have a ball from my major league debut.

One special memory I have that you can't put a price on is when my father came from Louisiana to watch me pitch in the Astrodome. I had a great game, and he saw that. It was the only time he came to watch me pitch in the majors. I really liked the way he was treated in Houston and at the game by the Astros. People came by to make sure everything was okay. It was announced that he was there via the public address system. He had never been treated in such a fancy manner, especially by white folks. I was grateful for that. He enjoyed himself and he talked about how much he enjoyed it. It was near the end of a season, and he was going to come back, but it never got arranged.

My father worked at night a lot and he never saw me pitch in high school. He worked and he wasn't always home when I was. There wasn't a lot of affection and hugs when I was growing up. You ate and went about your daily routine and went to bed. But that one night I pitched in Houston when he was there, I knew my father was proud of me.

21

Tranquility Along the Water

The J.R. Richard of the 2000s is a wiser man than the J.R. Richard of the 1980s. After surviving his hardships with some scarring, he has lived a very consistent life highlighted by the same things—his love of God, his love of fishing, his love of baseball, and his love of his third wife Lula.

Lula missed out on J.R.'s baseball career firsthand. She was not in his life when he endured the stroke and became homeless. Fishing is not necessarily her favorite sport, but J.R. is her favorite man, and she shares his powerful belief in the Lord. "Most people would be bitter about what happened," she said. "The thing is, when you place your trust in God, you have to know God for yourself, not just because somebody told you that God would do this and God would do that. You have to internally know it. Once you internally know God, there is no other way but the right way, and that is not to have animosity or any anger toward the Astros or whomever. So I can understand why J.R. doesn't have animosity toward them.

If he hadn't known God, yes, he probably would have, and most people would have."

Some former Astros, who have known J.R. a long time, feel they have witnessed changes in the man. Larry Dierker said he sees J.R at alumni functions and other Astros events at Minute Maid Park, but for some years Richard was absent from them. "He has been at peace with himself these last several years," Dierker said.

Ferguson Jenkins, who watched a young J.R. pitch in the National League, but who really did not get to know him until recent years, envisioned Richard as a 250-game winner before he retired. That was a milestone Richard never got to attain or challenge for because of his health problems. Taking a step back from looking at Richard the pitcher to viewing Richard the man, Jenkins remarked that J.R. had had an amazing life. "He's got a unique story to tell," Jenkins said.

There are times when J.R. thinks he might move away from Houston, back to Louisiana where he still has family and friends and roots. He imagines having a garden filled with collard greens, peas, and okra, "the whole nine yards" as he likes to say. He would spend his time fishing and hunting, but there is no Major League Baseball closer to Ruston, Louisiana, or more convenient to attend than Houston. When he pauses to think about it, baseball is still part of his life, though not as a player. Being an ex-player in the city where Richard played still carries some pleasant perks from the opportunity to participate in team events, to watching games in person, to mingling with old friends and teammates. And not very far from Houston, the fishing is pretty darn good.

J.R. Richard

I have never recovered 100 percent from the stroke in the sense of being 100 percent strong the way I was when I was pitching for the Astros. I still have to take some pills. My reflexes are not as good on my left side. If I have a long day, I get fatigued. My voice starts to slur a little bit. My wife, Lula, tells me that when I do get fatigued you can hear some slurring. I don't complete my sentences. I cut my sentences off. She pays close attention. I am not aware of this when it starts to happen. One thing that I do is try to stay active. I walk. I love to fish and hunt. I don't want to get out there in some godforsaken place and have something happen to me and not have the physical attributes or condition to get back home.

I have always loved fishing. I love to be in the outdoors. I love to be on the water. I love when the fish fight at the end of the hook and, if I am fishing alone, I love to spend the time relaxing and thinking. It takes between 30 minutes and an hour to get to a good fishing spot from where I live in Houston. I like lakes, rivers, bays. I fish for white bass, catfish, crappie, and speckled perch. It's a good variety of fish.

One thing I would like to get is a pontoon boat with a barbecue pit on it so while I am out fishing I can be cooking ribs. I would barbecue up some meat before we left the dock and I could lay it on there and keep it warm. It would be ready to eat when we were ready to eat. Or maybe a houseboat would be better. You can fish into the night and then go inside and go to sleep.

I go to Lake Livingston State Park often. You can rent boats for half a day. I like to go with a guide but not all of the time. Oh man, when the white bass start running, they run from all of the creeks to the lake. It's a spawning frenzy. They feed on the surface. You can throw anything out there. When you catch them, they fight hard. Sometimes they go down hard, and you have to get up from your chair, and the water is just churning. If you go out there to deeper water, you'll catch bigger fish like striped bass.

Even in the warm water of summer, you can catch fish, but the best thing is to go out at night. Put some lights on the boat, go out there with your deck chair, and sit down. They congregate. If you have a little light, they are drawn to it, and then the big fish come in. Bait your hook with a minnow and drop it to the bottom. You can catch fish of 40 pounds. Livingston is a good lake. I have caught a lot of fish on that lake. I've had a lot of fun on that lake.

There have been some different chapters in the book of my life. Baseball was very important, and I really felt fulfilled when I was pitching well. But it's all over. It's done. It was fun doing it. It's in the history books. You can't change history. So it's always there what I did in baseball. People can say what they want about my pitching, but the history books will always remain.

Pitching was always my thing, even in high school when I could hit. The pitcher is about 75 percent of the game. Nothing happens until he throws the ball. Good pitching can shut down good hitting. That's what makes a good pitcher worth his weight in gold. The pitcher is the most important player on the field. He has to throw it for anything to start happening. In the beginning I was a little bit nervous. I had some shyness. After your first few pitches, you're okay, especially if you throw a strike.

From the start I think being in Houston was an asset to me because it was so close to Louisiana. I was only 19 and I was pretty close to home. I always got chances to travel back. They also have great fishing around Louisiana, places that were not far up the street. Fishing was great relaxation for me when I was playing. It was a great getaway. There can be a monotony during the baseball season. It's a long season, and you play 162 games after spring training and then maybe into the playoffs. You need a change once in a while, and for me that was fishing. Usually you only get one day off a week, a Monday or a Thursday.

Some people couldn't stand the summer heat and humidity, but I liked to perspire and feel the heat. It kept me loose. I always liked the heat better than the cold. If it was 97 degrees, that was a good day for me. Of course, even though it's hot and humid in Houston for months, we played home games indoors at the Astrodome so it didn't really matter what the weather was like outside. I grew up with the heat in Louisiana, and heat wasn't any factor for me. But around me more people like to go fishing at night than during the daytime because it's so darned hot in Texas.

Just like baseball was part of my life, being homeless was part of my life and I can't just forget it happened. It's part of me. The stroke was the cause of a lot of things. I didn't even realize how depressed I got and how much the depression dictated my life. All of the time that I was sitting around in the house on the couch watching television and gaining weight, I kept thinking, *Now what am I going to do? What am I going to do next?* I wanted a new career and I called some of the guys that had been around me in the business world to seek employment.

I didn't feel like being around baseball, so I wanted to try something else. But for a while there, the stroke still had hold of me. It didn't allow me to do things physically that I needed to do on jobs. After my stroke some things really just disappeared. I don't have the same memory for details that

I did before it happened. I have weakness sometimes. My stamina is not the same. It should be, but it's just not there. Baseball really did help me, that emergency assistance, which carried me over to my pension. And baseball is still helping me now because I do personal appearances and autograph shows.

I hear some people say that I am an inspiration because I came back from the stroke and I came back from homelessness. Americans like to see their athletes come back from challenges. That's why they have a Comeback Player of the Year award in baseball. Americans want to see other people succeed who have had a hard time. Part of that is because they would like to think that if they had a hard time they could come back from it, too. Or they just admire you for doing it because they don't think they could cope in the same situation. They like to see the Phoenix rise from the ashes, the fall from grace, and the comeback, and all of a sudden you're on top again. People love that because the story is a tearjerker at the low point. I guess that pretty much describes my life.

Any time that I give a talk, I do talk about the bumps, bruises, and in-between in my life. You always keep your head up. My message is that you can be your own worst enemy. Don't let anything hold you back. The only thing that can hold you back is yourself. So don't make excuses. If you don't change, nothing in your life will change. Don't blame other people if things aren't going like they are supposed to go. Don't look at other people; always look at yourself. Eliminate other people and you can see what went wrong and how you screwed it up. People have to find themselves. They have to look inside of themselves to see what the real problem is. Even though we don't have all of the answers for the world's problems, to change the world you have to change yourself. Everything starts with you.

I do meet people who are bitter about something that happened to them 40 years ago. They haven't found the truth. They haven't found the testament. That's no way to be. That does not jell with me in terms of being happy and content. Life is always great. There are things out there you can be depressed about. But I have found contentment within myself. My thing is to keep going forward and not let the devil into my circle. How you deal with terrible things is up to you. People's highs and lows are different. My low, of course, would be sleeping under a bridge. The whole purpose for a day might be to keep warm…Being homeless and forced to live under a bridge is a mind changer.

I used to be more into money, but money isn't everything in life. You always hear people say that having their health is the most important thing. I definitely learned that. Having a stroke was God's decision. I couldn't stop it and I couldn't change it. I always have to tell people that I am not bitter. I hope they believe me. I have told people that over and over again because they can't believe it. They feel that I should be. But my life belongs to God, and I am living because he let me stay alive. You can't be bitter about that.

Epilogue

J.R. Richard and wife, Lula, live in a pleasantly appointed house in a quiet, neighborhood in Houston. Friends and business associates seem to drop by with some regularity. There is a king-sized barbecue in the average-sized backyard. J.R. loves to eat ribs and he loves to cook his own baby backs. A friend gave him a recipe that involves smoking them for five hours before indulging. Ribs may be Richard's favorite dinner main course. At the least they are near the top of the list. Before partaking of those slow-cooked ribs at Richard's house, those at the table hold hands and pray together, thanking God for the bounty of the meal.

One thing about living in Houston that remains a convenience, just as it was when he was a 19-year-old going off to the pros for the first time, is that it is only a five-hour drive to Ruston, Louisiana, cutting through Shreveport. Numerous members of the Richard clan still live in Ruston. In addition to Richard's periodic road trips to the old neighborhood and visits to old friends, family reunions are held there. Richard does not make the drive to eat ribs, but he does make the journey to say hello to people who have known him since he was a schoolboy. His Louisiana past is strong in Richard. It's a place where loved ones loved him and still do and where he developed the baseball skills that took him on a remarkable journey.

Wearing a loose fitting shirt in the oppressive steamy heat and a Houston cap with an oil derrick decorating it, Richard climbed into his gray, half-ton Silverado with appropriate leg room for a man of 6'8" for the ride east. A temporary, renewable handicapped tag hung from the rearview mirror. Richard slipped on a pair of glasses. He may be in his 60s, and have considerable gray flecking his hair, but J.R. also has a full head of hair and looks younger than his age. Before backing out of the driveway Richard offered a prayer for a safe journey. The radio, set to one of his favorite stations, discussed religious matters. "I gain a lot by listening to it," Richard said. "A lot of people don't understand the magnitude of God until he's brought you out of something."

If anyone would be surprised to see the handicapped parking tag, it has been granted because J.R. does not walk great distances nearly as freely as he used to do. "I still get pains in my legs," he said. "I have to park up close. No question I'm not 100 percent. I still have effects from the stroke. People say I recovered really well, but I'm in the 90 percent range of recovery, not 100 percent. My left side is weaker. If I do something physical, I have to rest in-between before I do anything else. It's something you deal with."

One of the people Richard has on the day's agenda is Coach Robert Smith, the man who guided his early days in sport. "I consider him a mentor," J.R. said. "He made things plain to us. He had a good attitude and he taught you to have a good attitude. He stressed education. He told us that sports are not the only thing in life. Sooner or later you're going to need that education."

J.R. was a prize pupil, but he was still a teenager, and that meant sometimes the coach had to give him a talking-to. "He had an authoritative voice," Richard said. "He had been around. He was young in age and old in knowledge and he had a kind heart. You know how you do crazy stuff when you're young? He could identify with a young athlete."

Richard was blessed with considerable athletic skills, but even the best athletes need to harness and direct their talent. Smith helped him do that from the time he was a sophomore in high school until he signed a contract with the Astros. "From [high school] on, he was influential to me," Richard said. "At that time I didn't know anything about the sport. I had athletic ability. I thought I could be the best. Coach Smith told me, 'You can be better than what you are.'"

This was August, and it was a quickie, one-day trip to Ruston, but family reunions are often in October when Richard stays around for a couple of days. "You see as many relatives as you can," he said. "Ruston will always be a part of me. I think of it fondly and emotionally. Growing up I was taught to respect your elders. It certainly developed character. It was part of growing up and becoming a man."

As he spoke, Richard chewed gum. He keeps an ample supply in the glove box in the truck to keep exercising those mouth muscles. He developed the avid chewing habit as therapy after the stroke. The effort worked, and—conscious that sometimes after long days he can be susceptible to slurring words—Richard still regularly chews the gum for the strengthening benefit. Richard's cousins are dotted around Ruston, and if he walks around town at all there is a good chance he will bump into a relative, friend, or someone who recognizes him. "There's always a good possibility," he said.

Sometimes Richard lets his mind roam and wonders what it might have been like to attempt to play two professional sports the way Bo Jackson and Deon Sanders did. But he always adds that he has no regrets that he chose baseball over basketball and football.

In recent years the Astros have been one of the worst teams in Major League Baseball. In 2011 the Astros lost 106 games, in 2012 they lost 107 games, and in 2013 they lost 111 games. In 2014 they lost only 92 games, a measured improvement. And a close observer would admit that there are signs that young players might be on the verge of turning it around. That's the conclusion Richard has reached from watching games on television and from his regular visits to Minute Maid Park. "I can see the growth," J.R. said. "The guys are starting to believe in themselves. At some point you have to really push yourself to see how far you can really jump. It takes a period of time. Baseball is an individual sport, but you have to do things collectively. Jose Altuve is one of the smallest guys on the club, but he's doing great. But being small has nothing to do with your mind-set. You have got to have that good attitude and mental preparation."

Altuve, who is listed at 5'6", won the 2014 American League batting title with a .341 average. Richard likes the hitting potential of George Springer and Dexter Fowler, too, but he doesn't see any budding J.R. Richards on the mound staff. The 2014 Astros were outscored by almost 100 runs. "Of course, I'm on the outside," Richard said. "I'd have to be around the guys more to see their potential. They are trying. Like everything else, it takes time. They definitely improved over 2013 for sure."

The Astros, founded in 1962, have never won a World Series championship and have come close only once, losing to the Chicago White Sox in the 2005 Series. "They should not have been there," Richard said. "They kind of got in the back door, but the fact remains they were there. To be honest, it would have been great if they won it. It would have been a boost to the city."

One of the great issues that has become almost like a ping-pong match in recent years is the future of the Astrodome. It was once one of the most famous buildings in the world. Its use over the years has diminished so dramatically that many advocate simply blowing it up. Whatever the final disposition of the building, Richard will always carry nice memories from his experiences in the stadium that was his hometown field as a player. "For fans it was like being in the living room and sitting in nice, comfortable chairs," he said. "It was like watching the game on a much bigger TV screen. You couldn't get rained out. That was one thing about the Astrodome: you knew you were going to play whatever the weather. I remember one time there was so much rain before a game and so much flooding that nobody could get to the stadium. I think the Astrodome was one of the greatest places in the world to pitch, if not the best. The ball didn't really carry."

Although Richard is not as active as a preacher as he was when he wore a collar, he does still receive invitations to speak at churches. Much of what he talks about comes under the heading of personal testimony, his own story of being on top of the world of baseball, being struck down by a stroke, becoming homeless, and developing a closer relationship to God.

"It is a testimony, a personal story, and what the Lord has done for me," Richard said. "Sometimes you have 20 people listening. Sometimes you have 200 and sometimes more. I definitely had a case of nervousness when I started, but then as you do it more and more, you get the story down to a science. You get better and better at it. I always let them know I am a child of God. Most of the people listening to me have some awareness of my story from the newspapers, but they still want to hear it from you. It's more communal when it comes from you. It sticks to your ears more."

When he makes speeches, Richard does prepare with notes and a framework of what he plans to say, but he has also spoken enough, telling much the same story that he doesn't always have to refer to those notes so closely. He does have a slightly different version when talking to a group of church-going adults who are older than if he is speaking to a group of school kids or to young people at baseball banquets. Sometimes he even addresses kids in groups at Minute Maid Park. "I tell them to be who they are," Richard said. "I talk to them a lot about responsibilities and I try to teach them about life. I say, 'Don't wait until your mother tells you to take the trash out.' Or, 'You know when the lawn needs mowing.' And 'Clean your room.' I also tell them that it is up to them—what they do with their lives once they learn the tools of a sport or in the classroom. 'The ball is in your ballpark.'"

Richard frequently is heard at one function and then has word-of-mouth recommendations to other groups. His favorite speaking places are baseball camps because the audiences are made up of kids who like his sport. "It's something I really know about, and teaching is a part of giving back," J.R. said.

Richard enjoys his half-dozen or so appearances at sports memorabilia shows during the year and is always pleasantly surprised how many fans remember a guy who last threw a major league pitch in 1980. "You don't think of yourself based on what you used to be," Richard said. "There are a lot of guys out there who played much more recently than you did. Life goes on. You worry that you will go out there, and nobody will care, and you will get your heart broken, and somebody will tell you that you aren't worth a bag of chips anymore. But people have been very nice and enthusiastic and line up for my autograph."

It's a tricky thing, those sports memorabilia shows. The men who played Major League Baseball decades ago have moved on to other stages of life, but they all admit that being privileged to play the game was a special part of their lives. The key, in J.R.'s mind is to appreciate the baseball part of his life but recognize it no longer defines who he is. "As long as you've got your sanity and you still know who you are, it's okay," he said. "You have to realize what makes you successful is what's inside you, not what you did. Spiritually, it's what's inside you that counts. One reason that I think fans today know about me is the computer. They can look you up on the Internet and read your statistics and find out about you."

As Ferguson Jenkins said of Richard, he has a unique story. Those who study his background will not only absorb the numbers from his winning seasons and gaze in awe at those strikeout marks, but they will find out about the stroke, the homelessness, and the life comeback. If those things had not become part of him, then those young readers would have a marvelous buffet of statistics to ingest, but might not perceive the richness of the man's character. "If those things had never happened," Richard said, "I think it would be entirely different. A lot of things would be put in a different perspective. If I was never homeless, I wouldn't have met a lot of people. I wouldn't have gotten another divorce. I wouldn't have ended up preaching. Maybe that would have happened a little bit later on in life. But God had my life already planned. Your journey is going to take you to several places. It just may take you a different way than you expected. You may take a different way to grandma's house, stopping at a cousin's first, but you're still going to grandma's house."

The highway stretched before J.R. at the wheel of his big truck, even though it was not the path to his grandmother's house but to Ruston. There was not much traffic on the road and there wasn't very much to gaze at beside the road for long stretches, either, except for rural farms. When the "Entering Louisiana" sign became visible from the truck, Richard pointed to it, noting the dividing line.

The only big city on the road east was Shreveport, which has 200,000 people, and is the hub of Northern Louisiana, a completely different world from New Orleans, deep in the southern section of the state. It is more than 300 miles and five hours of driving from Shreveport to New Orleans, roughly the same distance as it is from Houston to Ruston. Shreveport is not the tourist town that New Orleans is. It is an oil town at the confluence of Louisiana, Texas, and Arkansas—and a place J.R. knows well. Shreveport was the closest big city when he was growing up. After Shreveport the ride to Ruston is in the home stretch. The cities are about 70 miles apart.

As talented an athlete as Richard was in those three major sports, and with a passion for hunting and fishing as well, he never bothered with golf. So many former baseball, football, basketball, and hockey players take up golf as a hobby after retirement from their principal sports that it seems it is almost required. It is a new challenge that takes them outdoors and it isn't as demanding on bodies that may have been injured along the way by torn ligaments.

About six years ago Richard decided to give golf a try after all. For one thing it opened up another social world with other ex-athletes, putting him on a list of participants for charities where the main method of fund-raising is a golf tournament. He is a regular at Jenkins' event, the Joe Niekro event, and some events that raise money for kids. So Richard's golf is mostly built around worthy causes. As anyone who has tried the game quickly realizes, golf presents a complex challenge and can often make a player crazy with missed putts and drives wide of the greens. "I decided to give it a shot and I liked it," Richard said. "I don't really practice. I'm not trying to get another career in golf. I have fun. I think I am a little less than an average player. I relieve stress instead of bringing stress on. I have not made a hole in one. I've come close a couple of times. I don't have one yet. I shoot in the low 80s sometimes. The other guys don't know I don't practice. When I was young, I was a natural bowler. I could make my shots curve into the pocket. But ever since I had the stroke, I lost the spin on my ball. I was pretty good."

After all of the years he has resided in Houston, J.R. has been contemplating a move from the city to the country. Lula is planning to retire from her school bus driver job in the near future, and then they will talk seriously about it. Richard will probably stay in Texas but within easy driving distance of Ruston.

In his mind the ideal setting for retirement living would be in a rural area where the couple might have a few horses and raise a few chickens. There would definitely be a pond for fishing. The plan is to stock it with crappie, black bass, and blue gill. That would be an inviting destination for kids, grandkids of his, or neighborhood kids because those kinds of fish can be caught easily, and it's important that kids not to be bored when they try fishing. Richard would make sure that from his land it wouldn't be hard to access good hunting grounds, too, a place where he might chase down deer and some rabbits—just as he did when he was a kid. "Whatever is in the outdoors, I'm there," Richard said.

Easing his foot off the accelerator, Richard took the Ruston exit from the highway and was almost immediately engulfed by gas stations, convenience stores, and fast food restaurants, none of which were in existence when he was growing up. Not far down the road was the campus of Louisiana Tech, a school Hall of Fame basketball star Karl Malone helped put on the national map. Baseball star Ralph Garr's family members still own a house in Ruston. Football Hall of Famer Fred Dean's family members still own a house there. Garr, who is in the Grambling Sports Hall of Fame, said he has a son who graduated from Louisiana Tech. "I go back for class reunions," Garr said of where he grew up. "I love that little town. It has been good to me. Coach Smith did a lot for all of us there."

Coach Smith's house was the first stop on Richard's itinerary. J.R. joked that Ruston was small enough that, "You'd have to be a real serious idiot" to get lost there. Then he turned one street away from Smith's house and had to laugh. He pointed a block away and said, "You see that house? Ralph Garr used to live over there."

The brick building that was Richard's old high school, Lincoln, is now a junior high. An old football field had vanished. Richard pointed to an area now dominated by woods and said, "That's where I first played baseball."

Coach Smith opened the door and effusively welcomed Richard. At 80 he still had the build of a sturdy ex-athlete. He has gone gray, including his mustache, but generally looks younger than his age. Smith keeps track of his boys who played and went on to do great things in professional sports and he has no shortage of material about J.R. He brought it out, spread open a scrapbook on a coffee table, and talked a little bit about his early impressions. "My wife and Rich were cousins," Smith said. "Nobody could touch Rich on the baseball field. When he came up, we went 27–0 and won the state championship. He had everything it took. J.R. was a heck of a football player. He could throw 75 yards on the run."

Smith's coaching history is divided into pre-integration and post-integration time periods or pre-1970 and post-1970. The local high schools merged, and he went from a head coach of all African American players to an assistant coach for a mixed race team. Some years later he became head coach at Ruston High, but without saying so directly, it is obvious that the best times in Smith's coaching life were pre-integration when he instructed athletes like Richard, Dean, and Garr. In its own way, life was less complicated. The racial tensions in the community were of a different kind when the schools merged.

Just like everyone else, Smith was stunned when J.R. suffered the stroke that incapacitated him and led to the end of his professional career. "All we could do was pray for him," Smith said.

The two men climbed into J.R's truck and drove a couple of miles across town to visit with Buddy "OK" Davis, the longtime local sportswriter who had been such an influence on the community. At 68 Davis had recently suffered a stroke of his own and was living in a rehabilitation facility. Davis lives in a room with walls heavily decorated with autographed pictures of favorite athletes he has rooted for and favorite athletes he has covered. It is a mini-museum. Despite his own setback and physical limitations Davis continues to bang out blogs and columns for the local paper—even if he types a little bit slower. His memory seems extremely sharp, and he has many vivid, fond memories of J.R. the superstar high school athlete in all sports. "J.R. could have picked his sport," Davis said. "I've never seen anybody as good as he was baseball-wise. The scouts showed up every time he pitched. He was imposing, of great physical stature. But he wasn't just big. You can be big and not use your talents. He used all of his God-given talent. He had the trifecta of sports talent—baseball, basketball, and football."

Davis, who is white, said that when he began writing sports in Ruston in the 1960s, he received complaints when he covered stories about black athletes. "When people said that to me," Davis said, "I said, 'This conversation is over. They are going to be in the newspaper.' Racism really angers me. Every once in a while someone is going to let you know they're not crazy about blacks, which is a low-down shame." Before J.R. and Coach Smith left the rehabilitation center, Richard gave some advice to Davis about working hard on his rehab. Who would know better? Then they all held hands in a circle and prayed.

Richard believes there is still racism in baseball to some extent, though there have been large numbers of African American managers since the first in Frank Robinson with the Cleveland Indians in 1975, large numbers of coaches, and there are more minority front office officials than ever before. He is dismayed, however, that African Americans currently make up only about 8 percent of major league players. That makes him suspicious. "There is something going on," Richard said. "They can say that black athletes aren't playing ball, but I've always thought the black player had to be three times better, and that's the way it is. Why would there be discrimination? Why does the sun come up?"

Although Richard did have a career long enough to win 107 games, he knows he did not have enough time at the top to warrant Hall of Fame inclusion. The one honor he still hopes to receive in his lifetime is for the Astros to retire his No. 50 uniform. "I would like to see that happen," Richard said. "If it does, I'm going to be a happy man."

After visits with Smith and Davis, Richard stopped in at the school administration building to visit a longtime friend and then aimed the car back toward Houston, a 300-mile drive still facing him. He had enjoyed his little touch of home.

Retired number or not, Richard believes that coming back from the stroke, outlasting being homeless, and finding a fresh connection to God, means that despite the setbacks that would have completely crushed another man that his life has recovered. "This is a real happy ending," Richard said. "Going to heaven will be a happy ending. That will be the happiest of all endings."

Acknowledgments

Thanks to former teammates, friends, coaches, and family for helping to make this book possible.

Also thanks for assistance to the Houston Astros sports information office for its cooperation and for providing valuable material.

As always, a thank you goes out to the National Baseball Hall of Fame Research Library in Cooperstown, New York, for providing information.

And a special thank you goes to Don Hancock in Anchorage, Alaska, for helping to bring us together for this project.

Sources

Much of the material collected in this book is firsthand from J.R. Richard interview sessions at his Houston home as he relayed his compelling story.

It was supplemented with numerous contemporary newspaper accounts of J.R.'s pitching career that were included in Richard's file at the Baseball Hall of Fame Research Library.

The majority of these stories came from the *Houston Chronicle*, *The Houston Post*, and *The Sporting News*. In addition, articles from *The New York Times*, *New York Post*, the *New York Daily News*, Field News Service, Gannett News Service, *Los Angeles Times*, *The Washington Post*, *The Christian Broadcasting Network*, United Press International, and the Associated Press were studied.

Personal interviews were conducted with former Houston Astros players Enos Cabell, Jose Cruz, Larry Dierker, and Johnny Edwards. Interviews took place with Hall of Famer

Ferguson Jenkins; former Atlanta Brave Ralph Garr, who is from J.R's home town of Ruston, Louisiana; Robert Smith, J.R's high school coach; Buddy "OK" Davis, a longtime Louisiana sportswriter who followed J.R's career closely; and J.R.'s wife, Lula.

Information was collected from the National Alliance to End Homelessness and Move For Hunger (www.moveforhunger.org) and the Ultimate Astros website.

The book, *The Black Aces: Baseball's Only African-American Twenty-Game Winners* written by former big-league pitcher Jim "Mudcat" Grant, Tom Sabellico, and Pat O'Brien, was also consulted.